INNOVATION AT WORK

INNOVATION AT WORK

55 Activities to Spark Your Team's Creativity

Richard Brynteson, Ph.D.

American Management Association

New York • Atlanta • Brussels • Chicago • Mexico City • San Francisco
Shanghai • Tokyo • Toronto • Washington, D. C.

Bulk discounts available. For details visit:
www.amacombooks.org/go/specialsales
Or contact special sales:
Phone: 800-250-5308
Email: specialsls@amanet.org
View all the AMACOM titles at: www.amacombooks.org

This publication is designed to provide accurate and authoritative information in regard to the subject matter covered. It is sold with the understanding that the publisher is not engaged in rendering legal, accounting, or other professional service. If legal advice or other expert assistance is required, the services of a competent professional person should be sought.

Library of Congress Cataloging-in-Publication Data

Brynteson, Richard.
 Innovation at work : 55 activities to spark your team's creativity /
  Richard Brynteson.
  p. cm.
 Includes bibliographical references and index.
 ISBN 978-0-8144-3234-1
 1. Management—Technological innovations.   2. Creative ability in
  business.   3. Teams in the workplace.   4. Organizational change.   I. Title.
 HD30.2.B796   2013
 658.4′022—dc23   2012017450

Published by AMACOM Books, a division of the American Management Association.

The worksheets on the pages listed here have been adapted from other sources as follows: Worksheet #4 on pg 35, A Whole New Mind, adapted from *A Whole New Mind* by Daniel Pink. Worksheet #11 on pg. 69, Problem Solving Methodology, is based on work by The Creative Problem Solving Institute. Worksheet #13 on pg 119, Sources of Innovation, is adapted from *Innovation and Entrepreneurship* by Peter Drucker. Worksheet #14 on pg 125, The Ten Faces of Innovation, is adapted from *The Ten Faces of Innovation* by Tom Kelley. Worksheet #22 on pg 179, Criteria for Innovations, adapted from the video Tactics of Innovation by Joel Barker.

About AMA

American Management Association (www.amanet.org) is a world leader in talent development, advancing the skills of individuals to drive business success. Our mission is to support the goals of individuals and organizations through a complete range of products and services, including classroom and virtual seminars, webcasts, webinars, podcasts, conferences, corporate and government solutions, business books, and research. AMA's approach to improving performance combines experiential learning—learning through doing—with opportunities for ongoing professional growth at every step of one's career journey.

Printing number
10 9 8 7 6 5 4 3 2

Contents

Contents

PDF files for the Worksheets are available to purchasers of the book at:
www.amacombooks.org/go/InnovationWork

List of Worksheets

Preface

As the economy dramatically shifts and settles, fundamental questions are being raised about the readiness of the workers to handle the jobs of the future. Is your company ready to handle international competition? Is it agile enough to deal with rapid change? What skills will the new economy require?

- Traditional education with a focus on a proficiency in reading, writing, and arithmetic has worked in the past, but the new workplace requires more from its employees.

- Employees need to think critically, solve problems, innovate, collaborate, and communicate more effectively—and at every level within the organization. According to an *AMA Critical Skills Survey*, many executives admit there is room for improvement among their employees in these skills and competencies.

In an effort to assess how "top of mind" these skills and competencies are, the American Management Association (AMA)—in conjunction with P21, a national organization that advocates for 21st-century readiness for every student—surveyed 2,115 managers and other executives in AMA member and customer companies about the importance of the four Cs to their organization today and in the future.

This survey defined the most critical skills for organizational success as follows:

- Critical thinking and problem solving—the ability to make decisions, solve problems, and take action as appropriate;
- Effective communication—the ability to synthesize and transmit your ideas both in written and oral formats;
- Collaboration and team building—the ability to work effectively with others, including those from diverse groups and with opposing points of view;
- Creativity and innovation—the ability to see what's NOT there and make something happen.

For more information on the findings and a copy of the survey, visit
http://www.amanet.org/training/articles/3727.aspx

Purpose of This Book

The purpose of this book is to create centers of innovation. We are past the point where we can rely on brilliant or creative individuals. Innovation has to be organization-wide. Organizations have to build capacity for innovation so that they can produce innovation after innovation. This book presents ways to build that capacity. This book provides exercises and activities to build the innovation muscle of individuals, groups, and organizations.

It is my strong belief that innovation can be a learned trait by individuals, groups, and organizations. These exercises provide a roadmap, a method, an impetus to develop that trait.

How and Where to Use the Exercises

These exercises do not need to be used in any particular order. The time parameters do not need to be followed. They do not have to be followed verbatim. They can be plucked and harvested in any number of ways.

Some situations where these exercises may be used include:

- For standalone play during "lunch and learn" sessions at your organization.
- In organization-wide innovation training sessions.
- Strategically placed during process redesign sessions in order to shake up the thinking of participants.
- Peppered into fun events, such as scavenger hunts and company picnics.
- In problem solving, when tackling organizational problems head-on.
- As team-building activities for teams and groups.
- As activities for friendly competition between work groups.

In all cases, these exercises will help build the organizational innovation muscle.

Introduction—What Is Innovation?

Innovation is necessary for survival. This statement is true for individuals as well as for organizations. In order for us to be competitive as individuals, as organizations, and indeed, as a nation, we need to constantly add more value for our clients, customers, and constituencies. We do this through innovation. The innovation journey is fraught with obstacles. Naysayers line the route with catcalls, such as *"We tried that before"* and *"That will never work here."* Organizational potholes and boulders are strewn across the road. False starts and market shifts lead us down the wrong paths. Weariness from steep learning curves slows the process down.

The mountaintop is often enshrouded in the clouds of unending details, stops and starts. Distractions that are part of the day-to-day job tend to shift our focus over and over again. The journey is necessary, but doing a few important things will keep us going. Keeping close to the customer is central in this journey. Creating a culture of openness is also important for ongoing innovation efforts. A mindset of flexibility and inquiry is also helpful for developing and building on ideas. Creative collaboration is essential for moving teams forward toward market introduction.

So, what is innovation? One definition reads:

> Although the term is broadly used, innovation generally refers to the creation of better or more effective <u>products</u>, <u>processes</u>, <u>technologies</u>, or <u>ideas</u> that are accepted by <u>markets</u>, <u>governments</u>, and <u>society</u>. Innovation differs from <u>invention</u> or <u>renovation</u> in that innovation generally signifies a substantial positive change compared to incremental changes.

This definition is comprehensive and useful.

What innovation is:

- doing something significantly better
- creating a stream of new and useful products
- about making something better in order to improve the world, or make money, or both
- streamlining processes so that they are faster, cheaper, better, and more efficient
- revolutionizing entire industries
- facilitating creative change that will "woo" people
- leapfrogging the competition with products they had never thought of

This book is a call to action. If you ever thought that innovation was a ball in someone else's court, I hope that the exercises in this book prove you wrong. If you ever put off being innovative because you did not know what to do—you no longer have an excuse. If you ever thought that your organization needs to embrace innovation, now is the time. This book provides a roadmap.

The Structure of This Book

This book is broken down into four content areas and several addendums. Following are the principal chapters with exercises:

The Practice of Innovation

These exercises will immerse the participants in practicing to be creative and innovative. These exercises give participants shots in their arms and elevate their senses of innovation.

The Innovative Personality and Skill Sets

These exercises help build individual, group, and organizational innovation skills. They build individual capacity to be innovative.

The Culture of Innovation

It is one thing to develop a lucrative, one-shot innovation. It is another to build a culture that produces innovations on a regular basis. These exercises will help groups and organizations build capacity for ongoing innovation.

The Innovative Process

The process of innovation that is posited by this book contains five steps:

> Probing the Constituency
> Observe the Real Situation
> Develop New Concepts
> Converge and Build Prototypes
> Implementation

This set of exercises shows how to develop these five steps.

The content portion of this workbook is followed by two other sections:

Additional Questions, Posters, and Quotes

This section contains questions to ask during each stage of the innovation process. It also has quotes and sayings that can be posted up in an innovation room.

Cases

This section contains some innovation initiatives (caselets) from the author's consulting experience.

INNOVATION AT WORK

PART 1
The Practice of Innovation

❖ Forget, Unlearn, Dismantle ❖

🕐 *30–45 minutes*

Purpose   The purpose of this exercise is to help participants understand what the first steps in being innovative are.

Materials
- ✓ Flipchart paper
- ✓ Markers
- ✓ Imaginary dynamite

Procedure

1. Introduce the concepts of unlearn/forget/dismantle. This is always the first step in innovation. We must make a space for innovation. We need to let go of the old in order to make way for the new. More importantly, we need to let go of the old concepts that have been guiding our lives in the past.

2. Break the large group into smaller groups.

3. The groups will create one flip chart page (or two or three) that focuses on old concepts that we have let go of as a society. Brainstorm them with the participants and make sure there is a wide range of answers. Do this in order to "prime" the participants. For instance, some answers might include the following:

    a) The world is flat.

    b) Smoking is not bad for us.

    c) The only careers for women are in elementary education, nursing, and administrative positions.

    d) The Soviet Union is going to take over the world.

    e) China is a backward country.

    f) Telephones need cords.

4. Lead a discussion on what this brainstorm tells us.

    a) We may not be right all the time.

    b) Times change.

    c) What was right/appropriate/common knowledge/politically correct at one time may not be so any more.

    d) We can laugh at ourselves and our old concepts about the world.

5. Groups will create several flip chart pages on the wall. This time the topic will be what we can unlearn/forget/dismantle about our organization. (You might want to remind them of a ground rule like confidentiality.) You can prime them with statements like these:

    a) The old billing system works well today.

    b) Our only group of customers is _____ .

    c) The way we develop products is _____ .

    d) "Customer service" is a centralized function in our company.

6. **Optional:** Take one of the brainstormed options and focus on it (with a separate piece of flip chart paper). What actions would it take to dismantle that piece of the organization (or process) or rethink that customer group?

Debrief

- Your goal, as facilitator, is to get the participants to question, if not kill, the sacred cows in their organizations. You need to give them permission to unlearn and forget and dismantle.

- Often, in organizations, employees are stuck in the rut of "it has to be this way." It does not. Many successful organizations re-make themselves constantly in terms of new products, services, processes, and client bases.

- There may be nay-sayers in this group—"we have regulations," "we can't change anything because of corporate." You need to honor their voices while emphasizing what is possible to forget/unlearn/dismantle.

- Ultimately, you are giving them permission to look hard at all that they have held as "the way it is" in their organization.

❖ What if ? ❖

🕐 *45–60 minutes*

Purpose The purpose of this exercise is to engage participants in imaginative thinking. Innovation takes imaginative thinking.

Materials
✓ Flipchart paper
✓ Markers
✓ Wild-eyed imagination

Procedure
1. Reassure the group that "we're playing with ideas" in this exercise. Let them know that there are no wrong ideas, just interesting and engaging concepts.

2. Write "What if?" on several pieces of flipchart paper and invite the group to develop fanciful ideas. Start with more general concepts.

3. You might need to prime the group. For instance,

   a) What if half the days of the year were totally dark and half totally light?

   b) What if cars needed refueling every 10,000 miles only?

   c) What if you had to cut your food budget in half?

   d) What if you had to take in four foster children next week?

   e) What if the Internet went dead for one week?

   f) What if gasoline cost $7 a gallon?

   g) What if water cost $3 a gallon?

4. After 5–10 minutes of this fanciful thinking, choose one or two, and create a flipchart page for that one (or two).

5. Have the participants brainstorm the *implications* of that "what if?". Again, they can be fanciful. The wilder the answers, the better.

6. Do the same exercise for issues involving the participants' organizations. Do the "What if?" thinking and follow it with exploring the implications of one or two of the possibilities.

Debrief This is a fanciful exercise with no right or wrong answers. A debrief question might be, "What 'what ifs' do we have in this organization?" Where are we too satisfied and happy with what is rather than what could be?

❖ Innovative Connections ❖

🕐 *30–45 minutes*

Purpose   The purpose of this exercise is to force connections. Making obscure connections promotes innovative thinking.

Materials   ✓ Flipchart paper
   ✓ Markers
   ✓ Worksheet #1
   ✓ Open imaginations

Procedure   1. Divide the larger group into smaller groups of 4–7 participants.

   2. Hand out Worksheet #1.

   3. Ask participants to connect one item from the first column to one item in the second column and create a new product out of that connection. Have them do this with several of the items.

   4. When each group has 3 or 4 new products, have them report out with the larger group.

   5. List their mini-inventions on flipchart pages while everyone enjoys a good laugh at them.

   6. Ask each group to reconvene. Ask them to take two of the inventions from other groups and elaborate on them.

   7. After another 10 minutes or so, have a whole-group report-out.

Debrief   The wackier the product, the better. You are not trying to win product awards here, you are trying to inspire and build imaginations. This exercise can be used as a warm-up to more serious innovative thinking.

   Or, you might bring them directly into their own situation. Have them connect one of their existing products or services with an underserved market. What connections can they make now?

Worksheet #1
Innovative Connections

clothing washer	sock
coffee maker	machete
tire iron	iPad
trampoline	conveyor belt
cafeteria tray	carrot peeler
whiskey bottle	chip clip
Frisbee	baseball bat
Barbie doll	picture frame
bull whip	Legos
coat hanger	airplane wing
blender	door bell
kitchen chair	dog collar
volleyball net	microphone

Innovation at Work: 55 Activities to Spark Your Team's Creativity, Published by AMACOM Books
American Management Association, www.amanet.org.

9

❖ Levels of Innovation ❖

🕐 *60–90 minutes*

Purpose   The purpose of this exercise is to show how there are several levels of innovation available for any organization.

Materials
- ✓ Flipchart paper
- ✓ Markers
- ✓ Deep thinking
- ✓ Wild ideas

Procedure
1. Introduce the idea of "levels of innovation" below:

   - Process Improvement Ideas (lean manufacturing, Six Sigma)

   - Derivative Ideas (Starbucks, microloans)

   - Breakthrough Ideas (Harry Potter, space travel)

   - Radical Innovations (iPods, wireless)

2. Hand up eight flipchart pages around the room, two each for each of the four previous levels of innovations. For each level "Derivative Ideas" for example), add "past examples" for one of the flipchart pages, and "future potential ideas" for the other page.

3. Divide the larger group into four smaller groups. Have each group start at one "level," and brainstorm the past and the future of that level for the organization. Write down all the ideas they can think of that fit that "level" of innovation.

4. Time it for each group to be at each station for 10 to 15 minutes. Ring a bell, blow a whistle, and then tell them to move to the next "level." Do this until each group has spent a chunk of time at each level.

5. Tell participants that some ideas or products or services might fit into more than one of the levels.

6. You might have to put up more flipchart paper as each page fills up with ideas.

Debrief
- Ask participants how the process went for them. They probably wanted more time. There should have been much chatter during this period of time.

- Tell them that there is no rocket science that delineated exactly one level from another one.

- Suggest that organizations should be working at all levels. If there are limited resources, they must make allocation decisions. Regardless of those decisions, many people in an organization must think about what those "breakthrough" ideas might be in this particular industry.

- If you have time, you might look at organizations that are familiar to everyone—Target stores, a sports team, a grocery store chain, Starbucks—and talk about what the various levels of innovation might be in the future.

❖ Alternative Uses ❖

🕐 *10–20 minutes*

Purpose   The purpose of this exercise is to invite participants to think outside the box.

Materials
- ✓ Worksheet #2
- ✓ Bizarre sense of humor

Procedure
1. Divide the larger group into smaller groups of 4 to 7 participants.

2. Give each participant a copy of Worksheet #2.

3. Have groups develop lists of broken treasures.

4. Have smaller groups report out to the larger group.

Debrief   This is another fanciful, out-of-the-box exercise. The universe is full of gifts and surprises if we look for them. In third world countries, resourceful people use worn out tires for sandals and discarded bits of wire for shoelaces. They have to be innovative because of their lack of resources. We can learn to build that skill also.

Can you take this exercise further? What are the hidden resources in your organization? What do you discard that may be useful elsewhere? What are hidden treasures in some of the employees in your organization? What skills or insights might you be leaving on the table, discarded or ignored?

Worksheet #2
Broken Treasures

Think about the following "broken" items. What uses can you find for them? What value can you extract out of them? Also, you can combine any of these items.

Broken cement block

Torn Grateful Dead T-shirt

Broken alarm clock

Flat bike tire

Broken blender

Left shoe

Extra 2" x 4" pieces of lumber

Old matted feather pillow

Discarded swing set

Cracked mahogany salad bowl

Discarded metal flag pole

Tattered dog collar

10′ x 10′ piece of shag, green carpet

Sunken aluminum canoe

Discarded car seat

100 outdated, dog-eared books about the Crimean Wars

100 pounds of greasy ball bearings

Innovation at Work: 55 Activities to Spark Your Team's Creativity, Published by AMACOM Books
American Management Association, www.amanet.org.

15

❖ Jobs that Need to be Done ❖

🕐 *30–45 minutes*

Purpose   The purpose of this exercise is to help participants think like entrepreneurs. It helps participants look for market opportunities.

Materials   ✓ Flipchart paper
                ✓ Markers
                ✓ Acute understanding of fellow human beings

Procedure   1. Divide the larger group into smaller groups of 4 to 7 participants.

2. Give each group a target market of consumers that the organization serves. For example, it might be housewives or teens or retired people or busy young professionals.

3. Ask them to brainstorm the jobs "that the group needs to do."

4. Ask each group to present their findings to the larger group.

5. Have the groups move to the right or left and gather around a different flip chart and elaborate on the findings on that flip chart. Either they can add "more jobs that need to be done" or have them think of products or services that would help get these jobs done.

6. Have the smaller groups report out to the larger group.

7. **Example:** Say your group is stay-at-home moms. Your original brainstorm list might look like:

   a) Do the laundry while holding baby

   b) Prepare a meal while entertaining children

   c) Clean the bathroom

   d) Do the grocery shopping

   e) Clean the cupboards

   f) Arrange dental appointments

   g) Entertain toddler while nursing baby

   h) Keep living room clean

   i) Keep car clean and uncluttered

   j) Communicate with spouse

Debrief

- Invention is about seeing a need and plugging the hole. First, one has to start seeing the "jobs that need to be done."

- Ask participants to talk about some of their possible inventions. Ask others to elaborate on them. Ask what else is needed to make them marketable.

- Explain to them how cup holders in cars, home delivery groceries, and dog walking services all evolved from such an exercise. Also, think of the new generation of baby strollers. Originally, they were simple. Then, they were built with storage areas so that stuff could be carried with the baby. Then they needed to be compact in order to fit into car trunks so they got small again, but still with a storage area or two.

❖ A New TV Program ❖

🕐 *3–4 hours*

Purpose
The purpose of this exercise is to make innovation a game and help participants stretch their powers of creation.

Materials
- ✓ Flipchart paper
- ✓ Markers
- ✓ Quirky sense of humor
- ✓ Laptop computers with Internet access

Procedure
1. Divide the larger group into smaller groups of 4 to 8 participants.

2. Allow each group to choose a demographic/psychographic group:

   a) Tweens

   b) Teens

   c) Young adults

   d) Retired folks

   e) Stay-at-home moms or dads

   f) 18- to 24-year-old angry men

   g) Thirty-something rising professional

   h) Other

3. Have the smaller groups create a blockbuster new TV program for this group. Have them create major characters (with names), content, and a blueprint for the first three episodes. (The groups can use the Internet to research any of these subgroups.)

4. After three hours or so, check in with the groups and see if they are ready to report-out to the larger group. They can either use flip chart paper or create a PowerPoint.

Debrief
This is a fun exercise. Typically, participants are fully engaged in this process of creation. During the debrief, the facilitator might ask:

- At which points in the process did you feel fully engaged? Frustrated? Happy?

- How can you relate this exercise to your job?

- Where else do you research a group and then create something for them?

- Having done this exercise, will you look more closely at TV programs and see what they are trying to do and who they are aimed at?

❖ Storytelling ❖

🕐 *30–60 minutes*

Purpose   The purpose of this exercise is to build the storytelling skill set in participants.

Materials
- ✓ Notebook paper
- ✓ Pen
- ✓ Imagination

Procedure

1. Divide the larger group into smaller groups of 3 to 7 participants.

2. Tell them that their task is to create a compelling story and share with the larger class.

3. A story contains three major parts: action, conflict, transformation. Each of their stories should have these parts.

4. Tell the class some of your favorite stories and tell them why you like them. What makes a story powerful?

5. Each group can choose the subject of their own story. It can pertain to their organization but does not have to. These stories could be the basis for commercials, websites, or brochures. Examples of compelling stories include the following:

   a) The single mother who enrolled in your educational program, built, a career, and pulled her family off of welfare

   b) The recent immigrant who came to the United States penniless and used your social service agency to get a start in life

   c) The husband and wife who were constantly fighting until they bought an appliance that your company manufactures and how have nothing to fight about

   d) The dorky guy who could not get a girl, but now, wearing the suits your store sells, has plenty of social action

6. Have the groups work on the stories until they are reasonably polished.

7. Have them present the stories to the class.

Debrief   Lectures are boring; stories are compelling. Ask the class what makes a good story. Ask them what some of their favorite stories are. Dissect these stories with the class. What makes for an interesting story, a story that one wants to keep listening to? Which stories excite us and why?

❖ Love of Failure ❖

🕐 *30 minutes*

Purpose   The purpose of this exercise is to help potential innovators examine their attitudes toward failure.

Materials   ✓ Flipchart paper
                ✓ Markers
                ✓ Notebook paper
                ✓ Memories
                ✓ Worksheet #3

Procedure   1. Divide the larger group into smaller groups of 3 to 7 participants.

                2. Distribute Worksheet #3 and have the groups spend 5 to 7 minutes completing it.

                3. Debrief the answers with the larger group. What does this tell you about failure and success? Lead them to the point that failure and success are intertwined.

                4. Ask the participants to get into smaller groups again.

                5. Ask the participants to reflect individually on what failure meant in their families as they grew up (for 5 to 10 minutes). Ask them to jot down some notes, documenting some specific examples of their failures and how their parents, teachers, or siblings reacted.

                6. Ask the participants to share their list of failures and reactions with their smaller groups. One recorder in each group should write down themes that emerge from people's stories.

Debrief   The larger debrief should bring out the themes from each of the groups. The themes should be similar. Some people were punished for failures. Other people were encouraged to learn from them. Others were told to brush them under the carpet. How families deal with failures has a lot to do with how we deal with failure as an adult.

                Another part of this debriefing should address how we overcome our past programming and learn to deal with failure happily, successfully, and productively. Innovators need to embrace failure because most innovations are failures, at least at first.

Worksheet #3
Failures of Successful People

Please match the successful person in Column #1 to the failure in Column #2.

COLUMN #1	*COLUMN #2*
George Washington	three attempts to find the Northwest Passage
Walt Disney	903 light bulbs that do not work
George Macy	seven bankruptcies
Thomas Edison	6 out of 9 battles lost
Abraham Lincoln	47 times did not get off the ground
Wright Brothers	six bankruptcies
Thomas Jefferson	kicked out of the company he founded
Steven Jobs	lost six elections before being elected

Innovation at Work: 55 Activities to Spark Your Team's Creativity, Published by AMACOM Books
American Management Association, www.amanet.org.

25

Answer Key
Failures of Successful People

COLUMN #1	*COLUMN #2*
George Washington	6 out of 9 battles lost
Walt Disney	six bankruptcies
George Macy	seven bankruptcies
Thomas Edison	903 light bulbs that do not work
Abraham Lincoln	lost six elections before being elected
Wright Brothers	47 times did not get off the ground
Thomas Jefferson	three attempts to find the Northwest Passage
Steven Jobs	kicked out of the company he founded

❖ Visioning ❖

🕐 *1–2 hours*

Purpose   The purpose of this exercise is show the power of visioning and to give participants a concrete example about how to do visioning.

Materials
- ✓ Flipchart paper
- ✓ Markers
- ✓ Notebook paper
- ✓ Imagination (not optional)
- ✓ Computer projector with pictures of various vacant lots and playgrounds (optional)
- ✓ Laptop computers with Internet access (optional)

Procedure

1. Divide the larger group into smaller groups of 3 to 7 participants.

2. Ask the participants to close their eyes. Read them this passage. "You (a consultant) have been approached by a neighborhood group with a problem. The city has just purchased a nearby vacant lot. There are no other playgrounds anywhere near this plot of land. The group asked you to develop a physical layout for an ideal playground. In addition, because the city has no money for building the playground, the neighborhood group has asked you to develop a potential list of partners to help bring this project into being."

3. Members of the group might have questions. You do not have answers. They can choose the community and the plot of land.

4. Show slides of vacant lots and playgrounds, if you want. This might help their mental imagining.

5. Let the participants begin the task. Remind them that there are two discrete parts of the task. First, they have to mentally develop and sketch out the physical layout of the playground. Second, they have to create a list of potential partnerships and how these partnerships would fit together to accomplish the task.

6. After 1 to 2 hours, have each group present their plans.

7. **Optional:** The Internet access computers can be used to research potential partners.

Debrief   "Visioning" and "networking" are two key behaviors of successful innovators. Innovators have to be able to envision an outcome that they are trying to create. They are to have the imagination to envision that which does not exist. Most innovators also have to rely on other resources to bring their innovations to fruition. Who will be those partners? Who has the resources that they do not have? Who will be the angels to fill in the gaps to make this or that project happen?

- Possible partners for the playground development project:
- Nearby Home Depot or other building materials store may donate materials.
- PTA group may volunteer labor to help build.
- Trader Joe's usually helps neighborhood groups with projects like this.
- Kiwanis, VFWs, Elks, and other like clubs are likely to consider giving resources.
- Other neighborhood businesses are likely to support the project.
- Local sports teams are often looking for good publicity.
- Local college and high school students often have to build "service learning" into their curriculum. For instance, many high school students have to perform 40 hours or so of service work.

❖ Green Innovation ❖

🕐 *60 minutes*

Purpose The purpose of this exercise is have participants search for innovations within a certain industry—the green industry. Another purpose is to show participants that innovations build on each other.

Materials
- ✓ Flipchart paper
- ✓ Markers
- ✓ Notebook paper
- ✓ Pens
- ✓ Laptop computers with Internet access (optional)

Procedure
1. Divide the larger group into smaller groups. Participants can share computers. Each small group should have a scribe, a sheet of flipchart paper, and a marker.

2. Have each scribe divide the flipchart paper into two columns: **New Products** and **Possible Other Products.**

3. Have participants go to the website treehugger.com, trendhunter.com, or a similar green products–type website.

4. As participants peruse the website, have them call out to their scribe new, interesting products that they are noticing. The scribes should add these products to the first column. Upon hearing this call-out, others can brainstorm what further products might come about that are similar to or as a result of this product. The scribes should add these ideas to the second column.

5. As the sheets fill up, have the participants post them on the walls.

6. After 45 minutes or so, have groups walk around the room and look at the findings of the other small groups.

Debrief Hunting for trends is one of the first steps in innovation work. Trend hunting should not be limited to a person or two in marketing research. Because of the Web, anyone can and should be a trend hunter. Besides, trend hunting is fun.

The key phrase in this trend hunting process is "What might this innovation lead to?" or "What might be the next in line of this line of products?"

You might have a contest and give awards for the most interesting product, most likely to succeed product, and/or the most bizarre product.

❖ Practical Individual Creative Skills ❖

🕐 *30 minutes*

Purpose   The purpose of this exercise is to help individuals assess their own practical creative skills and to create an action plan for building those skills.

Materials
- ✓ Worksheets #4 and #5
- ✓ Pens
- ✓ Insightful self-assessment

Procedure
1. Divide the larger group into smaller groups that are manageable in size. It is preferable that the participants be in groups of people who know them well.

2. Hand out Worksheet #4 and Worksheet #5.

3. Explain to the group the premise and elements of Daniel Pink's *A Whole New Mind* (see Worksheet #4).

4. Tell the group that their task is to critically assess their own skills in the arena of practical creativity. Have group members help assess your capabilities in each of these areas.

5. Have group members help develop action steps to develop your skills in this area. What activities would help you build these skills?

6. Each participant should report to the larger group one or two action items that they intend to take to build these practical creative skills

Debrief   Daniel Pink's work *A Whole New Mind* is excellent and worth the read. His premise is that many left-brain type jobs can be either sent to India or computerized and therefore employees need to develop their right brain skills in order to survive the marketplace. These skills are listed on the worksheet. These are clearly right brain skills, and sometimes are harder to train for. According to Pink, employees should be trained in these skills more than the usual left brain skills.

Worksheet #4
A Whole New Mind

Premise: We should be educating our students more in the right brain. Left-brain jobs will be taken by computers or lower paying locations. Below are six ways to educate youth for the work of tomorrow.

Design

It is no longer sufficient to create a product, a service, an experience, or a lifestyle that is merely functional. Today it is economically crucial and personally rewarding to create something that is also beautiful, whimsical, or emotionally engaging.

Story

When our lives are brimming with information and data, it is not enough to marshal an effective argument. Someone somewhere will inevitably track down a counterpoint to rebut your point. The essence of persuasion, communication, and self-understanding has become the ability also to fashion a compelling narrative.

Symphony

What's in greatest demand today isn't analysis, but synthesis—seeing the big picture and crossing boundaries, being able to combine disparate pieces into an arresting new whole. This is also called systems thinking.

Empathy

The capacity for logical thought is one of the things that makes us human. But in a world of ubiquitous information and advanced analytic tools, logic alone won't do. What will distinguish those who thrive will be their ability to understand what makes their fellow woman or man tick, to forge relationships, and to care for others.

Play

In work and play, there is need for play. The current younger generation has been brought up on computer simulations and learns well in this mode. In addition, there is ample evidence that there is enormous health and professional benefits of laughter, lightheartedness, games, and humor.

Meaning

We live in a world of plenty. We can now pursue more significant desires: purpose, transcendence, and spiritual fulfillment. In addition, with all of the information available, our job now is to make meaning of what is present.

Innovation at Work: 55 Activities to Spark Your Team's Creativity, Published by AMACOM Books
American Management Association, www.amanet.org.

35

Worksheet #5
Practical Creative Skills

CREATIVE SKILL	CURRENT STRENGTHS	ACTION STEPS
DESIGN		
STORY		
SYMPHONY		
EMPATHY		
PLAY		
MEANING		

Innovation at Work: 55 Activities to Spark Your Team's Creativity, Published by AMACOM Books
American Management Association, www.amanet.org.

37

PART 2

The Innovative Personality and Skill Sets

❖ Inquisitiveness ❖

🕐 *15 minutes or more*

Purpose   The purpose of this exercise is to build the participants' skills in asking questions and building curiosity.

Materials
- ✓ An object
- ✓ A burning sense of curiosity
- ✓ Worksheet #6

Procedure

1. Divide the larger group into smaller groups of 4 to 7 participants. This can also be an individual exercise.

2. Distribute Worksheet #6.

3. Give participants a "thing" to examine. This might be an orchid, a pine tree, a potted plant, a car, an air conditioning unit.

4. Each person or group has to develop a list and of 25 questions about the item. The questions can be practical or whacky or anything in between. Help the participants by giving them sample questions. For instance, for the pine tree, questions might include:

   a) How many birds have nested in you?

   b) Have you witnessed any murders?

   c) Do they put Christmas lights on you?

   d) What is the most interesting conversation that you have overheard?

   e) How does photosynthesis work?

5. Have the participants return to the larger group and ask each participant to share one or two of their questions.

6. If this is just a warm-up exercise, have the smaller groups go on to the task at hand and develop the 25 questions for their topic.

   a) For instance, this author was once working with a military group trying to reduce the testing time for a hydraulic system for a large piece of equipment. We started by asking 25 questions about the hydraulic system.

   b) For instance, this author was once working with a television station, trying to develop new programming. We started by asking 25 questions about our target demographics (stay-at-home mothers, for instance).

Debrief   Curiosity is the imperative for innovation. If you wish to be more innovative, start by being inquisitive and asking questions about the world. Recent research suggests that the most innovative executives are the ones who ask the most questions. Great creative geniuses have always asked questions. Leonardo da Vinci found shells at the top of a mountain in Italy and asked why. He also asked why birds could fly and other such "mundane" questions.

Worksheet #6
25 Questions

Build your curiosity by asking questions. Develop 25 questions on a topic: a tree, an on-boarding process, social media, whatever.

1. _____

2. _____

3. _____

4. _____

5. _____

6. _____

7. _____

8. _____

9. _____

10. _____

11. _____

12. _____

13. _____

14. _____

15. _____

16. _____

17. _____

18. _____

19. _____

Innovation at Work: 55 Activities to Spark Your Team's Creativity, Published by AMACOM Books
American Management Association, www.amanet.org.

43

20. _____

21. _____

22. _____

23. _____

24. _____

25. _____

Innovation at Work: 55 Activities to Spark Your Team's Creativity, Published by AMACOM Books
American Management Association, www.amanet.org.

❖ Building Networks ❖

🕐 *60 minutes*

Purpose The purpose of this exercise is to give participants practice in building networks, which is a key trait of innovative leaders.

Materials
✓ Flipchart paper
✓ Markers
✓ Laptop computers with Internet access
✓ A global vision

Procedure

1. Divide the larger group into smaller groups of 3–7 participants.

2. The task of each of these groups is to create a "ghost hunting" business. The parents of Baby Boomers are dying off and Baby Boomers desire to communicate with them. You, the would-be proprietor, have always been fascinated by ghosts. You have played around with ghost hunting paraphernalia. You have gone on ghost tours in New Orleans. You have read many books about them and have even thought that you have spotted one or two.

3. If you were going to give this business your best effort, what networking would be useful for you? What organizations would you connect with and/or form partnerships with to build a pattern of success? How might you use social media tools to build this business? Create a media strategy to build your network of success.

4. Have the groups spend 30–45 minutes searching the Internet for organizations and people who are engaged in ghost searching, ghost running, ghost exposing, and ghost busting.

5. Have the small groups report-out their media and networking plans to the larger group.

Debrief   The groups should have some fun with this exercise. The key learning includes the following:

- Successful innovators know how to network with the right organizations and people.

- They know what the holes in their skill and resource sets are and know that they need partners to fill them.

- Networking is more than a coffee or a lunch; it is a series of mutually beneficial activities and arrangements. For instance, if you create a blog, you might want to mention someone else's similar blog. You might want to mention other organizations of interest to ghost hunters, for example, on your Facebook page.

The key to social media success is getting the buzz about you going in other organizations. It is creating an ecosphere around, for example, ghost hunting with you at the center. This requires intensive networking.

❖ The Rebel ❖

🕐 *60 minutes or more*

Purpose The purpose of this exercise is to get participants to feel comfortable in challenging the norms and assumptions at their organizations.

Materials
- ✓ Flipchart paper
- ✓ Markers
- ✓ Worksheet #7
- ✓ Invisible sword and shield

Procedure
1. Tell the group that this exercise is often called "assumption testing." Explain that the best and most innovative managers are constantly testing and challenging the norms, assumptions, and status quo.

2. Divide the larger group into smaller groups of 4 to 8 participants.

3. Distribute Worksheet #7 to the participants for use in this exercise.

4. Ask each group to develop a list of two to three deeply held assumptions.

5. Ask them to challenge those assumptions, one at a time. What if they were not true or necessary? If these assumptions were not true, what could we do differently? What if they could be reversed? What if the opposite were true? Each group should develop a list of implications as if the assumptions were not true. What could be the upside of some of these implications?

6. If the groups are having a hard time thinking about deeply held assumptions, here are some ideas to spur their thinking:
   a) Employees have to be at their desks to be good workers.
   b) Employees have to have suits and ties on to be considered professional.
   c) The only people who want our products are over 50 years old.
   d) We need an internal HR department.
   e) We should not hire people without college degrees.

7. **Variation:** This exercise can be tailored for different groups. For instance, if the group consists of design engineers for autos, some assumptions that may be tested are:
   a) Cars need four wheels
   b) Cars have to cost more than $10,000
   c) Steering wheels need to be round

Debrief   It is often difficult to convince employees that they will not be shot if they challenge deeply held assumptions. Just because we challenge the roundness of steering wheels does not mean we are going to immediately change them. Fanciful, bizarre ideas can often lead to productive ones.

It is important to get employees to push the boundaries of traditional thinking. Innovation rarely happens inside narrowly defined lines. Big, game-changing innovations occur by taking big leaps.

Worksheet #7
Assumption Challenging and Testing

"Assumptions are maintained by the hug of history. Yet, history does not guarantee their validity, nor does it ever reassess their validity."

—Michael Michalko

Thus, we must challenge their validity. In this segment, we will challenge the validity of important organizational assumptions.

Blueprint:

1. State a challenge:

_____

_____

_____

_____

_____

_____

2. List your assumptions:

_____

_____

_____

_____

_____

3. Challenge your fundamental assumptions:

_____

_____

_____

_____

_____

_____

Innovation at Work: 55 Activities to Spark Your Team's Creativity, Published by AMACOM Books
American Management Association, www.amanet.org.

49

4. Reverse each assumption. If you can, write down the opposite of each one:

5. Ask yourself, how might I accomplish each reversal?

6. Obtain as many differing viewpoints as you can:

Innovation at Work: 55 Activities to Spark Your Team's Creativity, Published by AMACOM Books
American Management Association, www.amanet.org.

❖ Personality Trait: The Next Box #1 ❖

🕐 *60 minutes*

Purpose The purpose of this exercise is for participants to see that being innovative often requires "get into the next box" thinking rather than "out of the box" thinking.

Materials
- ✓ Flipchart paper
- ✓ Markers
- ✓ Worksheet #8

Procedure

1. Ask the larger group what they think the phrase "getting outside the box" means. Discuss why that phrase is so popular.

2. Ask what "getting into another box" might mean. How might this process be different? How might one "get into another box"? You might ask, "What other boxes are worth getting into?"

3. You might give examples of organizations that have gone into another box for ideas:

   a) The Bellagio Hotel management went to Italy for ideas on how to innovatively decorate a hotel.

   b) The Rainforest Café management went to a rainforest to build a theme for their chain of restaurants.

   c) The Minnesota Department of Corrections consulted with Target stores to figure out a way to inventory their convicted but released felons.

   d) The Como Park Conservatory personnel went to Japan for ideas on how to design a meditative garden.

   e) Howard Schultz, founder of Starbucks, hung out in Italian coffee bars while developing his idea for Starbucks in the United States.

4. Divide the larger group into smaller groups of 4 to 7 participants. Give the participants a copy of Worksheet #8. Ask them to work with one of their organizations or divisions/departments of their organizations to brainstorm what they might be able to learn by going into one of the "boxes" on the worksheet. Or they can think of other boxes (not on the worksheet) to visit and glean ideas from.

5. After 30 to 45 minutes, ask each group to report out an interesting idea or two.

6. **Optional:** Have the participants get back into their small groups. After having heard the ideas from the other groups, ask each participant to claim one high value "box" that they intend to visit in the next six months that might give them valuable ideas.

7. The smaller groups will report out these ideas to the larger group.

Debrief   This is one of the more difficult exercises because it stretches cognitive abilities.

The main point of this exercise is innovation is not just about creating something entirely new. It is about taking someone else's idea and adapting it to your circumstances. You do not need to "reinvent the wheel" in order to be innovative. Look what Schultz of Starbucks did. Coming up with a completely new product often requires engineers, but this kind of "getting into another box" requires just curiosity, acute observation, and seeing with new eyes.

Some of the processes or events on Worksheet #8 will have no relevance for the organization in question. Some of them might have connections. It is important to get the participants to stretch their imaginations in order to make the connections.

Worksheet #8
Other Boxes

Starbucks coffee delivery system

UPS package delivery system

University student registration system

Target store's return policy system

Marine Boot Camp

Disney World (or another amusement park)

McDonald's food delivery system

House-building process

Art museum preservation, selection, and display

Minor league baseball entertainment system

NFL draft process

Senator or governor selection, campaign, or election process

Funeral/memorial service, burial process

Roller coaster operation

Golf course management

Cruise ship management

Scavenger hunt

Boston marathon event planning

Library management

Preparing a Thanksgiving dinner

Getting child ready for first day of first grade

Innovation at Work: 55 Activities to Spark Your Team's Creativity, Published by AMACOM Books
American Management Association, www.amanet.org.

53

❖ Personality Trait: The Next Box #2 ❖

🕐 *60 minutes*

Purpose
The purpose of this exercise is to give participants another method to get into another productive box.

Materials
- ✓ Flipchart paper
- ✓ Markers
- ✓ Laptop computer with Internet access (preferably 2 or 3 per group)

Procedure
1. Ask the larger group what they think the phrase "getting outside the box" means. Discuss why that phrase is so popular.

2. Ask what "getting into another box" might mean. How might this process be different? How might one "get into another box"? You might ask, "What other boxes are worth getting into?"

3. You might give examples of organizations that have gone into another box for ideas.

   a) The Bellagio Hotel management went to Italy to look for ideas on how to innovatively decorate a hotel.

   b) The Rainforest Café management visited a rainforest to build a theme for their chain of restaurants.

   c) The Minnesota Department of Corrections consulted with Target stores to figure out a way to inventory their convicted but released felons.

   d) The Como Park Conservatory personnel visited Japan for ideas on how to design a meditative garden.

   e) Howard Schultz, founder of Starbucks, hung out in Italian coffee bars while developing his idea for Starbucks in the United States.

4. Divide the larger group into smaller groups of 4 to 7 participants. Ask each group to develop a list of five "things" that they would find interesting to understand better. These "things" could be machines or processes or systems. Each group should have access to the Internet. Ask them to go to the website www.howthingswork.com. Call up their list of "things" and study how they work. Take notes on each of them.

5. Ask them to brainstorm what they might be able to learn by going into one of these "boxes." After 30–45 minutes, ask each group to report-out an interesting idea or two.

6. **Optional:** Have the participants get back into their small groups. After having heard the ideas from the other groups, ask each participant to claim one high value "box" that they intend to visit in the next six months that might give them valuable ideas.

7. The smaller groups will report out these ideas to the larger group.

Debrief   The debrief for this exercise is similar to the last one. Once this author was working with a military group and trying to find a faster way to test a hydraulic system. We studied other hydraulic systems in www.howthingswork.com and were able to bring those findings into our problem at hand.

Innovators are curious. They are interested in the way things work. If you are not naturally curious, you probably will not be a natural innovator.

❖ Personality Trait: The Next Box #3 ❖

🕐 *1–3 hours*

Purpose   The purpose of this exercise is to help participants naturally get into another box in order to be more innovative.

Materials
- ✓ Flipchart paper
- ✓ Markers
- ✓ Post-it Notes
- ✓ Vivid imagination
- ✓ Worksheet #9

Procedure
1. Divide the larger group into smaller groups of 4–7 participants.

2. Ask each individual to focus on a business dilemma/problem/challenge/ situation that warrants some focus. They might want to write these down on Post-it Notes.

3. Hand out Worksheet #9.

4. In the smaller groups, have one member present their business problem. Have the group choose a "forced associate" from the list on the worksheet.

5. Have members of the group list attributes of that "associate." For instance, if they choose "garden," they might list:

   a) Flowers grow there

   b) Deer eat the broccoli

   c) Basil smells good in autumn

   d) Needs water, mulch, sun, and good soil

   e) Sometimes blighted by beetles and bugs

   f) Some plants might overcome others

   g) Ground might dry up

   h) Attracts bees in august

   i) And so on

6. Have group members connect the problem at hand with the association. For instance, they might say, "Our sales shortfall is like the garden because . . ." Make as many associations as possible. These connections might bring to light some solutions to the problem. Keep making the connections even if they seem far out or weird or laughable. You never know when a spark lands in the right place.

7. After the groups have tackled a couple of these problems, run a larger group "debrief."

Debrief

This exercise is called forced association because it forces participants to make connections. It is not optional. The connections may see extreme or silly at first but may yield some valuable insights. These people have presumably tackled these problems for many hours before this exercise. They have probably used linear, left-brain thinking to solve them, without success. This exercise takes them into nonlinear, right-brain, creative thinking that may be more productive, given the chance.

When conducting the debrief, help the group see the connections and honor those connections even though they might not yield a practical solution, *at this point.*

Worksheet #9
Forced Associations

Garden

Bar

Amusement park

Restaurant

Professional sports contest (baseball, football)

Vineyard

Mountain village

Shopping mall

Innovation at Work: 55 Activities to Spark Your Team's Creativity, Published by AMACOM Books
American Management Association, www.amanet.org.

59

❖ Design an Experiment ❖

🕐 *30–60 minutes*

Purpose　　The purpose of this exercise is to give participants practice in designing experiments.

Materials
- ✓ Notebook paper
- ✓ Pens
- ✓ Flipchart paper
- ✓ Markers
- ✓ Laptop computer with Internet access

Procedure
1. Divide the larger group into smaller groups of 4–7 participants.

2. Talk with participants about the importance of experimentation in the innovation process. Only when we test our ideas do we get an idea of how good they might be.

3. Have each group choose processes from one of their organizations—a process that might need improvement.

4. Have the smaller groups design experiments around these processes to test new ways of doing them.

5. At each experiment, participants should ask, "What are the unintentional consequences of this procedure?"

6. For each experiment, ask, "What can be learned from this experiment?" "Would the results be the same if we rolled it out to a larger audience?"

7. Have the smaller groups explain their experiments to the larger groups and have all participants ask clarifying questions.

8. Ask participants what it would take to run these experiments.

Debrief　　Car companies smash cars into walls to see how crash test dummies survive the impact. Banks set up test branches with innovative layouts to see how customers react. Pharmaceutical companies test out new drugs to see if they work and what side effects may emerge. Then they tweak the ingredients. A *Harvard Business Review* article from the 1980s was entitled "Staple Yourself to an Order." The article suggested that we should all test the procedures that our customers use in doing business with us.

Experiments, and especially failed experiments, can breed innovation. The point is—keep experimenting. You do not know how it will turn out.

❖ Building Innovation DNA into Your Life ❖

🕐 *30 minutes*

Purpose   The purpose of this exercise is to build a plan for individuals to become more innovative in their personal and work lives.

Materials
- ✓ Worksheet #10
- ✓ Pens
- ✓ Imagination
- ✓ Discipline

Procedure

1. Distribute Worksheet #10 to participants.

2. Re-emphasize to the participants how it is important to hold yourself accountable for becoming more innovative.

3. Briefly explain each of the five behaviors associated with Innovation DNA. These five are from the book *The DNA of Innovation:*

   a) **Experimenting:** How to continually conduct experiments in order to improve products and services. Experiments can be simple or complex.

   b) **Questioning:** Get in the habit of asking questions. Like a child, ask why the sky is blue, why fish swim, or why people have two eyes.

   c) **Observing:** In what situations can you be more observant? Observing deeply customers, clients, your products being used, or your competition in action?

   d) **Networking:** You do not have all the keys to the kingdom. Other people, organizations, companies, think tanks, and task forces hold pieces of truth that may be useful to you. Who are these people?

   e) **Associating**: This is not technically a behavior, but a thinking pattern. It is, however, a muscle that can be built. How can you make new connections? Coffee shop and bookstore, car and cup holder, or gourmet food and home delivery.

4. For the first part of this exercise, individuals work alone, quietly trying to fill in Worksheet #10. Ask them to create specific action steps for each of these behaviors. For instance, they may decide to build the habit of asking questions in a specific task force meeting. Or they might go to a specific commercial location and watch their company's product or service being used.

5. After about 15 minutes, have the participants share their tactics with one or two other people in the larger group. Hearing the action steps of others might spur on more possible action steps of their own.

6. For the larger group, have each individual share one of their action steps.

Debrief   Innovation is not magic or fluff. Sometimes it is just plain hard work. These are behavioral muscles that we—that is, anyone—can flex. It is a matter of practice and being okay with getting it wrong at times. The point is to try it. The point is to observe differently. The point is to ask more questions. The point is to be more curious about one's life.

Worksheet #10
Building Your Innovation DNA

INNOVATION DNA BEHAVIOR	ACTION STEPS
Experimenting	1. _____ 2. _____ 3. _____ 4. _____
Questioning	1. _____ 2. _____ 3. _____ 4. _____
Observing	1. _____ 2. _____ 3. _____ 4. _____
Networking	1. _____ 2. _____ 3. _____ 4. _____
Associating	1. _____ 2. _____ 3. _____ 4. _____

Innovation at Work: 55 Activities to Spark Your Team's Creativity, Published by AMACOM Books
American Management Association, www.amanet.org.

65

❖ Creative Problem Solving ❖

🕐 *60 minutes*

Purpose   The purpose of this exercise is to give participants practice in using an effective creative problem solving approach.

Materials
- ✓ Worksheet #11
- ✓ Worksheet #12

Procedure

1. Hand out Worksheet #11 and Worksheet #12.

2. Divide the larger group into smaller groups of 3–5 participants.

3. Have each person write down a problem or challenge in his or her life. Using the worksheets, each participant should work through this problem or challenge with the help of their group members. Their group members should coach them through each step using the guidelines from the worksheet. Allow each person 10–15 minutes.

4. At the end of an hour or so, invite any participants to share the results of the process.

Debrief   This process is used throughout the world. It gives a good framework for working through problems in an organized way.

Worksheet #11
Problem Solving Methodology

- **Objective Finding**
  - *Purpose:* To single out a goal or objective and set its priority
  - *Task:* Develop a list of problems/challenges to work on; settle on the juiciest one
  - *Process question:* What are we really trying to create here?
  - *Outcome:* An aim, general object, or common goal

- **Fact Finding**
  - *Purpose:* To use all of our senses and feelings to deeply examine the objective before selecting important information
  - *Task:* Find out what everyone knows or needs to know about the objective including how they feel about it
  - *Process questions:* Who? What? When? Where? How? What don't we know?
  - *Outcome:* A broad base of information

- **Problem/Challenge Finding**
  - *Purpose:* To seek many new ways to perceive people, situations, and challenges and opportunities from a diverse perspective and to choose the best one
  - *Task:* Generate a variety of problem statements worded for idea stimulation
  - *Process question:* In what ways might we...?
  - *Product:* A single, clear action-oriented problem statement

- **Idea Finding**
  - *Purpose:* To generate alternatives, possible solutions, interesting approaches
  - *Task:* Define and identify the necessary conditions for brainstorming
  - *Process questions:* Substitute? Adapt? Modify?
  - *Product:* An abundance of alternatives, potential solutions, diverse ideas, and creative approaches to problem

- **Solution Finding**
  - *Purpose:* To measure, rank, and examine possible solutions
  - *Task:* Generate a list of criteria for use in evaluating the selected ideas
  - *Process questions:* What needs must be satisfied for the problem to be solved?
  - *Product:* A priority of approaches for solving the problem; choosing a working solution.

- **Acceptance Finding**
  - *Purpose:* To identify assistance, objections, acceptance needs, and resources to gain commitment
  - *Task:* Generate all the steps needed to implement the solution.
  - *Process questions:* Who? What? Why? When? In what ways might we (IWWMW) gain acceptance?
  - *Product:* A plan of action with times, dates, people, places, and tasks

Innovation at Work: 55 Activities to Spark Your Team's Creativity, Published by AMACOM Books
American Management Association, www.amanet.org.

69

Worksheet #12
Creative Problem Solving

Objective Finding	
Fact Finding	
Problem Finding	
Idea Finding	
Solution Finding	
Acceptance Finding	

Innovation at Work: 55 Activities to Spark Your Team's Creativity, Published by AMACOM Books
American Management Association, www.amanet.org.

71

❖ Brainwriting ❖

🕐 *30–40 minutes*

Purpose The purpose of this exercise is to show participants another method for generating a large number of ideas in a short time.

Materials
- ✓ Blank sheets of paper
- ✓ Pens

Procedure

1. The room should be set up so that 10 or 12 participants can be seated around a common table. Depending upon the size of the group, there might be more than one table.

2. Introduce the concept of brainwriting. Participants probably understand the concept and rules of brainstorming, the process of capturing many ideas out loud in a group setting. Often the most vocal and fast-talking participants get their ideas out there, and quiet, slower but perhaps more thoughtful participants sit quietly. Brainwriting, in contrast, is a silent activity. It allows quiet and more verbal participants to have equal footing in the idea production realm.

3. Each individual should have a blank sheet of paper in front of him or her. Each table should have a problem or a challenge statement. Assign these or have people at the tables decide which issue they wish to work on. Make sure that the tables do not spend too much time on this part of the process.

4. Once the problem/challenge has been decided upon, the groups can start the process. Each person should write down one solution on his or her piece of paper and then push the paper to the center of the table. Then they should take a piece of paper that another person has written an idea on and write another idea under theirs. Then they exchange that piece of paper for another one and do it again.

5. The other ideas written on the page should spark other ideas. Some ideas might build on the other ideas; others might emanate from random thoughts. If the sheets fill up, provide another blank one and collect the full one.

6. Call a halt to the activity at any time.

Debrief Ask for participant reactions to the process. Did it work for them? How did it differ from brainstorming or other processes? Did they feel that they were more fluid with their ideas or less fluid? Was the silence strange? When might they use this process?

GAME/SIMULATION

Assessment
The problem-solving game 1

"Not again!" exclaimed Raul Desjardins, a group vice president, as he arrived at work and opened his office door to discover his prize Ming dynasty Chinese vase in pieces on the carpet in front of his desk. "I'm not going to let the night cleaning staff in here . . . I'll start closing my door when I leave at night. In fact, I'll lock my office."

Three months ago, Raul had lost a Limoges figurine the same way; it was on the book shelf that hung on the wall next to his office door, and he had arrived to find the figurine broken on the floor. Luckily it was in two pieces, so he could cement it together. When Raul took it home to mend, he replaced it with the Ming vase; he purchased it in Hong Kong and decided that it would serve just as well on the wall shelf. His office had at least a half dozen pieces displayed at any one time—pieces from different parts of the world, with a colorful story to go with each. And now the Ming vase was in a hundred pieces.

The first time something broke, Raul said nothing to the cleaning staff; mistakes happen, and the figurine can fortunately be mended. However, with this morning's repeat occurrence, Raul immediately called Mr. Morello, the manager of building services, and summoned him to the office. "We'll take action to avoid future problems of this type," he thought, as he awaited Mr. Morello's arrival.

1. What do you think is Raul's objective in having objects of art in his office?

2. What is the problem? What are the likely causes?

3. What evidence do you have?

4. What should Raul have Mr. Morello do?

GAME/SIMULATION

The problem-solving game 2

When Mr. Morello arrived, he could see that Raul Desjardins was annoyed. And he could see a vase in pieces on the carpet—the obvious source of his annoyance.

"Look here. This vase cannot be replaced or mended. Your staff should know better than to dust a priceless object of art such as this." Actually the vase was not a priceless object at all, but a reproduction; Raul had paid under $50 for it, and knew where to get another. But a principle was at stake, and he wanted to make his point with Mr. Morello.

"You're absolutely right, Mr. Desjardins. I'll have a talk with my people tonight when they come on. We'll make sure that they don't dust any of your things on that shelf," Mr. Morello promised. "We can do even better than that," Raul added. "I'd rather they didn't clean my office. In fact, I'll secure my door at night. It may be like locking the barn after the horse is stolen, but it will at least solve the breakage problem." Mr. Morello agreed and promised to send someone in with a dustpan and brush to sweep up the fragments. They parted, and Raul replaced the vase with an inexpensive Delft ginger jar that was on the windowsill.

5. Do you agree with what Raul and Mr. Morello decided to do? Why?

6. Do you see any alternative ways of dealing with the situation? How can such an accident be prevented in the future?

GAME/SIMULATION

The problem-solving game 3

That evening, Raul Desjardins was working late at the office. The cleaning staff began to vacuum the floor and clean up. One of the women stuck her head in Raul's office and said in broken English, "We are sorry you lost your vase, sir, but I know we are not to blame. We never touch the beautiful things on your shelf. But just the same, we are sorry."

Raul thanked her. Then she asked if he would like her to empty his waste basket. He said yes, but began to wonder later if that was a good idea, since he had told Mr. Morello that the cleaning staff shouldn't touch his office.

Disturbed with himself (or with the cleaning lady for being so apologetic) and distracted by the noise level of the vacuum cleaner outside his office in the reception area, Raul Desjardins got up from his desk, crossed the room to the wall with the bookshelf, and pushed the door closed. Two seconds later—on his way back to the desk—he heard the door slam, followed by a rocking sound on his wall bookshelf. He turned just in time to see his Delft ginger jar come crashing down, scattering pieces all over the carpet!

7. Given this new information, what changes do you want to make (if any) in your statement of the problem?

8. How do you recommend dealing with the problem in light of your new evidence?

9. How can the problem be avoided in the future?

10. What new insights do you have about the problem-solving process now that you have gone through this exercise?

The problem-solving game

Now that you have gone through the ten questions, it's time to compare your answers with ours. There are ten points for each question. Thus a perfect score is 100. On each answer, decide in your group how well you handled the question and give yourself the appropriate credit: from 0 or 1 point, up to a full credit of 10 points. Enter your score in the box in front of each answer.

1. We must begin by identifying (or inferring in this case) Raul's objective in having art objects in his office. We have evidence to suggest that they serve as "conversation pieces" that give Raul opportunities to tell colorful stories about his travel experiences. They might also serve as a constant reminder of his chief pleasure: international travel. The fact that he had "at least a half dozen pieces displayed at any one time" suggests that he rotates his artwork and thus supports this second objective (the "constant reminder").

2. What called attention to the fact that Raul is losing some of the decorative pieces he bought on his travels is that he discovers them broken when he walks into his office. He thinks the reason they are breaking (problem) is that the night cleaning staff was being clumsy. But there are other likely causes: for example, vibration of the building or of the wall on which his book shelf is mounted.

3. Raul has no evidence that the cleaning crew is breaking his art objects. He knows that the breakage is occurring at night. We do have evidence that he leaves his office door open when he leaves at night but that it is closed when he arrives in the morning (first paragraph). This is hard data.

   We also have evidence that the shelf is on the same wall where the door is located, and we might suspect a connection. Since doors do not close of their own accord, we conclude that someone is closing his door at night. The cleaning people? The night watchman making his rounds? The person who operates the vacuum cleaner (who might be closing the door in order to vacuum behind it)?

   In short, Raul has no evidence that the cleaning people are responsible for the breakage. In fact, his Delft ginger jar and his Ming vase were placed elsewhere in the office and had never been broken. If he suspects that the cleaning people are dropping his art objects, why would they only do so when dusting things on the wall shelf, and not on the windowsill or side table?

4. Raul might ask Mr. Morello if he has any idea how the art objects are getting broken, and he might ask Mr. Morello if someone on his staff can pick up the pieces and vacuum the rug. But he should not assume that the cleaning people are to blame. He has no evidence either that they are, or are not, responsible.

5. There is nothing wrong with isolating a suspected cause to see if the problem is reduced or eliminated. This is the basis of troubleshooting. However, this can be done without accusing the cleaning staff. Raul can simply tell Mr. Morello that he prefers not to have his office cleaned. Or he might simply lock the door when he leaves, assuming that the cleaning staff does not have a key. But we don't agree with the way Raul handled it. He put Mr. Morello on the spot, and made it likely that Morello will scold the night crew.

☐ 6. Yes, there are alternative ways of addressing the problem. Recall that a problem is anything that prevents us from achieving an objective. If Raul's objective is to present himself as a world traveler and art collector, he can meet this objective without placing breakable objects on display; paintings, bronze figures, wood carvings, masks, etc., would meet this objective, and there would have been no problem of breakage. However, if you took Raul's problem to be "breakage," then the solution is to anchor his art objects in place (e.g., by placing adhesive or rubber cement on the base).

☐ 7. We now have new evidence to indicate that the root or cause of the problem is a vibrating wall that shakes whenever the door closes with force. The breakage of his art objects must now be seen as a symptom of this problem of vibration.

☐ 8. If we are correct in our belief that Raul's objective is to have "conversation pieces" and mementos of the pleasures of travel, then one way to eliminate his losses is to place unbreakable objects on the shelf (e.g., artifacts made of metal, stone, and wood). This would solve the problem without identifying the cause. On the other hand, suppose Raul's objective is to display porcelain or pottery. We have evidence to support this possibility: all three objects of art were ceramic. In this case, one way to eliminate his losses is to place these objects on wider surfaces (e.g., desk top or coffee table) where they won't be affected by the vibration.

☐ 9. Given that the vibrating wall is the root cause of the breakage, Raul could do one of several things to avoid future breakage:
   - Keep breakable objects off the wall shelf, or cement them down with adhesive.
   - Have the vibrating wall braced so that it remains sturdy when the door slams.
   - Install a closing mechanism on his office door so that door closes gently.
   - Display non-breakable objects of art that will still meet his objective of showing where he has been and stimulating conversation.

☐ 10. There are two major insights that might emerge from this exercise. First, we, like Raul, tend to assume cause without subjecting our thinking to close scrutiny and acid tests. We tend to see symptoms (breakage) as the problem, and thus do not dig deep enough to find the root causes (vibrating wall). Secondly, when faced with a problem, we, like Raul, are not aware that we lack evidence. In the other cases used to teach problem solving, all the information is present in the case study. But in this exercise, as in real life, evidence may be lacking. And yet we can't afford to wait until a fortuitous happenstance (Raul's slamming door) provides us with the missing link—the piece of evidence that we lacked but didn't even know we were missing. Such is the real world when we embark on the problem-solving process.

☐ After entering your score in each of the boxes, add up the ten scores and enter the total in the box to the left. As noted earlier, a perfect score is 100. A score of 85 or better reflects a high degree of sophistication in avoiding the potholes of assumptions and fuzzy thinking that lie along the road a problem solver must travel.

❖ Analytical Thinking Test ❖

A Self-Assessment Exercise

Directions: There are two parts to this exercise. In Part One, you'll be reading five situations, each followed by four conclusions. Some conclusions are true (T), some are false (F), and some are questionable or cannot be made without further information (?). Beside each conclusion, indicate which applies by placing an X over the appropriate answer.

PART ONE

1. According to the police in the suburban town of Maplewood, the automobile accidents occurring during the workweek (Monday through Friday) are 250% more numerous than those occurring during the weekend (Saturday and Sunday). We can conclude that:

   A. Traffic at commuter hours is probably contributing to the higher workweek accident rate............................. | T | ? | F |

   B. Accidents are as likely during the workweek as on the weekend... | T | ? | F |

   C. It's more dangerous for you to drive during the workweek than on weekends in Maplewood................. | T | ? | F |

   D. Maplewood may not be a commuter community... | T | ? | F |

2. George is a recent MBA who wishes to spend a year working overseas. He understands that the newly independent nation of Rotunda needs MBAs, both in government and private industry. Salaries are paid in Rotunda Dollars (RD). The range paid to MBAs is from 7,000 to 21,000 RD per annum, depending on experience. Half the MBAs earn less than 14,000 RD and half earn more than 14,000 RD. From this we conclude that:

   A. The average salary of MBAs in Rotunda is 14,000 RD .... | T | ? | F |

   B. A normal distribution (bell-shaped curve) seems to apply here .... | T | ? | F |

   C. The chances are 50-50 that George will earn more than 14,000 RD in his first year............................ | T | ? | F |

   D. MBAs in Rotunda typically earn between 12,000 and 16,000 RD .... | T | ? | F |

3. A group of surveyors who wanted to find out the fuel oil consumption for residential heating in 1985 throughout the state of Pennsyltucky interviewed a representative sample of homeowners by telephone in early 1986, asking the following question: "What would you say is the average monthly amount of fuel oil used to heat your home last year?" The results yielded a statewide average of 47.3 gallons of No. 2 fuel oil per month. From this we know that:

A. The question should have asked for the annual amount of fuel oil used to heat their home .... | T | ? | F |

B. Telephoning people and asking them to guess is a poor way to obtain the desired information .... | T | ? | F |

C. The average Pennsyltucky home will require about 567.6 gallons of oil for heat in 1986 .... | T | ? | F |

D. Apartment dwellers were excluded from the survey.. | T | ? | F |

4. A major automotive dealership mailed a questionnaire to all customers who had purchased a new car within the prior year. The questionnaire asked, among other things, whether they would like to have received a free check-up every 5000 miles during the six months following purchase. Of the 27% who responded, 68% stated that they were in favor of having a free check-up. From this we can conclude that:

A. A majority of new car owners who had purchased through this dealership favored having a free check-up.. | T | ? | F |

B. With regard to the sample, the number of respondents may be adequate, but their representativeness may not be .... | T | ? | F |

C. The dealership believes that free check-ups during the half year following purchase of a new car are desirable .... | T | ? | F |

D. The percentages would probably have been different if the survey had involved respondents who purchased two or more new cars .... | T | ? | F |

5. Grassmaster, a lawn mower manufacturer, must select a supplier of paint that will dry within 20 minutes of spraying. Two vendors have been identified for consideration: A and B. Paint from A dries slower than B's paint at normal room temperature (68°F). But at temperatures of 90°F and higher, A's paint dries faster than B's. Both dry at the same rate when equal amounts of Agent X are added to the paints during the normal manufacturing process. Agent X is already present in B's product as part of the normal manufacturing process, but not in A's. From this we can conclude that:

A.	Grassmaster could buy A's paint as normally manufactured and add Agent X before spraying it in order to shorten the drying time	T ? F
B.	Two factors affect drying time: heat (room temperature) and Agent X...	T ? F
C.	As long as Agent X is present in paint, the drying time is reduced. The amount is unimportant.................	T ? F
D.	Agent X exerts a greater influence on drying time than does room temperature...	T ? F

PART TWO

Directions: There are three proposals (A, B, and C) stated below. You are to select one of these three and develop a list of all the advantages and disadvantages (pros and cons) of implementing it, as well as all the interesting points associated with the proposal (further information to be obtained before or after the proposal is acted upon). Complete the table on the next page for the proposal you select. Go for quantity—the more entries you have in each column, the better will be your chances of thinking clearly when you decide whether to recommend that the proposal be accepted or rejected. Here are the three proposals, from which you should now select one and complete the table on the next page.

A. Proposed: That state laws be passed requiring that a man and a woman desiring to marry must first announce their engagement in the local newspaper and then live together for a minimum of three months before applying for a marriage license.

B. Proposed: That all young men and women be required to serve one summer in the army in military training; this requirement would be to serve for 10 weeks at any point between their 17th and their 20th birthday.

C. Proposed: That each citizen of the country receive from the government a plastic laminated identification card containing their photo, signature, and identification number (Social Security number in the U.S.), to be carried or worn at all times.

After selecting the proposal you will be thinking through, develop your list by using the table on the next page.

ADVANTAGES	DISADVANTAGES	INTERESTING POINTS

ANALYTICAL THINKING TEST

Answer Sheet

Directions: The correct answers are noted below, along with the reasons. Place a check mark beside every answer you got correct. There is a total of 20 points possible. Enter your score in this box...

PART ONE

1. Automobile accidents in Maplewood

   A. False. The accident rate is not higher during the workweek. Even if this is a commuter town (which we don't know), workweek accidents are as frequent as weekend ones... $\boxed{T \mid ? \mid \boxtimes}$

   B. True, since 250% is 2.5 times, and days are also 2.5 times as numerous in the workweek as on weekends.. $\boxed{\boxtimes \mid ? \mid F}$

   C. We cannot tell until we define "dangerous," which depends on when (hour of the day) and where (commuting, shopping, etc.) you're driving.................................... $\boxed{T \mid \boxtimes \mid F}$

   D. True. (It would also be true if the statement said that Maplewood might be a commuter community.) .... $\boxed{\boxtimes \mid ? \mid F}$

2. Annual salaries for MBAs in Rotunda

   A. We don't know this. If the distribution is normal, this would be true. But we cannot assume that income is distributed normally between 7,000 and 21,000 RD .... $\boxed{T \mid \boxtimes \mid F}$

   B. We don't know this. There might be two distinct income groups, new vs. experienced, natives vs. mother country, government vs. private industry (i.e., a "bimodal" distribution) .... $\boxed{T \mid \boxtimes \mid F}$

   C. This is not an issue of chance. George is a recent MBA, and pay is based on experience. George's first-year earnings are likely to be less than 14,000 RD .... $\boxed{T \mid ? \mid \boxtimes}$

   D. True if distribution is normal, false if distribution is bimodal. Since we don't know, we must question the statement .... $\boxed{T \mid \boxtimes \mid F}$

3. Fuel oil consumption throughout Pennsyltucky

   A. True. People are more likely to remember annual consumption than "average monthly." Also, the time of year of the survey may affect "monthly" estimates .... $\boxed{\boxtimes \mid ? \mid F}$

   B. True. Fuel oil distributors could provide more accurate information and with much less effort by the researchers.. $\boxed{\boxtimes \mid ? \mid F}$

   C. We don't know enough to forecast. The research is shaky, the weather varies, and the 12-times-multiplier can turn small errors into large ones.. $\boxed{T \mid \boxtimes \mid F}$

   D. True. Only homeowners were contacted. Some apartment dwellers might own their own apartments (condo, co-op, etc.), but some others don't own, making the statement true.. $\boxed{\boxtimes \mid ? \mid F}$

4. Free check-up for new car purchases

    A. If it had read "majority of respondents," then the statement would be true. But we need more than a 27% response to generalize to "majority of new car owners." ...... ☐T ☒☐F

    B. True. Each part is true. Even if the first part had read ". . . may not be adequate," it would still be true. Similarly, the second part is true whether it reads "may be" or "may not be." In fact, we have reason to suspect that the respondents are not representative, since those not interested in a free check-up are less likely to reply than those favoring it. .... ☒☐?☐F

    C.   It is risky to infer motives from the dealer's actions. Also, we don't know what "desirable" means. From a vehicle maintenance standpoint, yes (true). From a profitability standpoint, no (false).. ☐T ☒☐F

    D. False. The survey was not limited to purchases of only one new car. Those who purchased two or more new cars are already involved as respondents .... ☐T ☐? ☒

5. Grassmaster's need for fast-drying paint

    A. We don't know if adding Agent X after manufacture will have the same effect as adding it during manufacture .... ☐T ☒☐F

    B. True. There may be other factors that also affect drying time, but the statement is still true as it stands.. ☒☐?☐F

    C. We don't know if there are upper and lower limits to the amount of Agent X necessary for it to speed up drying time.. ☐T ☒☐F

    D. False. Room temperature (90°F) exerted a greater influence on drying time than did the presence of Agent X... ☐T ☐? ☒

Reminder: Count the total number of answers you got correct and enter this number in the box on the previous page. Then go on to Part Two on the next page.

PART TWO

There are no right or wrong answers to the exercise you went through. However, you should have come up with at least five advantages, five disadvantages, and two or three interesting points. These numbers should double when the list is expanded as a group activity. Here are our lists, with which you can compare your own.

A. Couples desiring marriage must first live together for three months:

ADVANTAGES	DISADVANTAGES	INTERESTING POINTS
1. Fewer surprises and risk of marriage not working.	1. Could lead some people to becoming "marriage samplers," living with different mates but never marrying.	1. What would be the view of the churches and religious leaders?
2. Reduced divorce rate.		2. Where would couples live together?
3. Couples learn how to live together in a relatively "fail-safe" environment—less pressure.	2. Buying or renting a home or apartment will be expensive if marriage doesn't materialize (leases are for more than three months).	3. What effect on abortion rate?
4. Fewer "passion" marriages.		4. What effect on divorce rate?
5. Eliminate marriages done for legal reasons and not for love (e.g., to gain entry to U.S., to qualify for an inheritance, etc.).	3. Some might enter it just to have a child more "legitimately."	5. Is three months enough to accomplish the purpose of the proposal?
6. Supportiveness of parents and friends can be determined and possibly influenced before marriage.	4. Psychologically damaging by creating "losers" who have been through several engagements without marriage.	
7. Psychology of "building toward" is more constructive than "after the honeymoon."	5. Difficult for some partners who know they want marriage now and cannot wait three months (e.g., military or student far away from their would-be spouse, dying person wanting to marry nurse).	
8. Young couples who don't understand implications and responsibilities of marriage would enter it with more maturity.	6. Couples who have grown up together ("the girl next door") and known each other for years shouldn't have to live together before marrying.	
9. Stimulates business in the apartment-rental industry.	7. If they make it through the tryout period, it's not necessarily smooth sailing thereafter.	
10. Public announcement of intent reduces the temptation to "play the field" during the months preceding marriage.		

ADVANTAGES	DISADVANTAGES	INTERESTING POINTS
	8. Unnecessary—couples who want to live together before marriage (or even without marriage) can already do so without any need to formalize or legalize the procedure. 9. Newspapers will become crammed with engagement notices—not very interesting reading. 10. Successful tryouts might lead couples to continue to live together and never marry.	

B. Youths would be required to serve one summer (10 weeks) in the army:

ADVANTAGES	DISADVANTAGES	INTERESTING POINTS
1. Eliminate the need for draft for longer period (1–2 years).	1. Disruptive to personal lives.	1. Would all youths get the same training for 10 weeks? Or would there be different tracks?
2. Develop physical and mental stamina, self-reliance, discipline, respect for authority, pride in serving country, etc.	2. Seen as curtailment of individual freedom.	2. Should they live on a military base, or could they live at home and commute to a nearby base?
3. Reaches many youth when they are least influenced by parents, teachers, and other "authority figures."	3. Expensive to give everyone a little instead of giving a few trainees a lot (breadth vs. depth).	3. Could efficiency of military training be improved, given the higher level of trainees?
4. Provides another set of role models for shaping values to live by.	4. Might require additional military bases, equipment, training cadre, etc.	4. How many people are we talking about each summer?
5. Enables youth of all socio-economic levels and sub-cultures to live and work together in a relatively fail-safe environment.	5. Would they really be combat-ready, or would they *think* they were fit to fight, especially against a professional, full-time army?	5. Would trainees be harassed or required to perform menial chores that might nogate many of the advantages?
6. Time (10 weeks) is long enough to effect permanent position change, yet short enough to not be disruptive to lives (education, career, marriage, etc.).	6. Hard to administer and determine at what age each youth will attend, and when.	
7. Give the country a trained citizen's army that is relatively combat-ready at any time; serves as deterrent to other nations taking military action against us.	7. Many weapons and defense systems are too high-tech to be operated by people who have only had ten weeks of basic training.	
8. Gives all youth an equal view of what a career in the military would be like, probably leading to more career soldiers.	8. Likely to create a caste system of "regulars" and "10-week wonders."	
9. Better quality of recruits than in present army.	9. Difficult administering the exceptions who are excused for such things as for physical or mental disabilities.	
10. Increase in patriotism, and a better informed electorate.	10. U.S. could become subject of international ridicule.	

C. Government issuance of a photo-signature plastic I.D. to all citizens:

ADVANTAGES	DISADVANTAGES	INTERESTING POINTS
1. Is highly reliable I.D. for check cashing, travel, etc.	1. More costly than I.D. number only.	1. How often would this be done—every 10–20 years?
2. Should reduce fraud and similar criminal acts.	2. People wanting "newer" photos every few years.	2. Where done—at Post Offices? Motor vehicle registries?
3. Is more personal than just a number.	3. Requires equipment (Polaroid camera, laminator).	3. Would people carry them? Would laws be necessary requiring this (like the wearing of seat belts)?
4. Makes census-taking more accurate.	4. Requires operators and training in how to operate the equipment.	4. How long would citizens have to wait during the initial "tidal wave" of issuing cards to every Social Security card holder?
5. Would establish drinking age reliably.	5. Cannot be done by mail— citizen must go to a center.	
6. Provides better control of illegal immigration.	6. Citizens annoyed by the inconvenience, the unflattering photo.	5. Could this be alleviated via alphabetic scheduling (e.g., all A through C names during the first two weeks of August, etc.)?
7. Time saved in establishing positive I.D. over one's lifetime should more than offset the time and cost of going in for a photo.	7. Replacement of lost cards a nuisance and expense.	
8. Police have an immediate check on drivers of stolen vehicles, contraband, etc.	8. Fraud still possible through makeup, wigs, eyeglasses, moustaches, etc.	
9. Could eliminate need for passports or visas to some countries.	9. Could add employees to government payroll instead of reducing costs.	
10. Government could charge and make money on it.	10. Some people change in physical appearance much faster than others.	

❖ TEST OF CREATIVITY ❖

A Self-Assessment Exercise

The left side of your brain handles analytical thinking: logical, rational, linear, numerical, precise. Many aspects of your job call for analytical thinking: planning a project, preparing a budget, learning a procedure, solving a problem, studying alternatives, and making decisions.

The right side of your brain handles creative thinking: expansive, visionary, intuitive, spatial, artistic. Whenever you come up with new ideas or create products, procedures, forms, programs, or plans that are new (or, at least, have never been generated by you before), you are drawing on the right side of your brain.

This self-assessment exercise will help you to get a quick measure of your creativity. There are fifteen questions. Each is timed. We suggest you get a kitchen timer or alarm clock or wristwatch, since you are likely to become absorbed in the exercises and forget to keep track of the time. Alternative: get a friend to be your timekeeper.

On each exercise, read the instructions. Then immediately start the clock.

1. **Five Minutes** In the space below (and on a separate sheet of paper if you need more space), list all the words you can think of that begin with the letter c. **Start timing now.**

2. The local soft drink bottling company has a fleet of trucks whose drivers make daily deliveries at the same supermarkets, drug stores, and beverage distributors. That is, the drivers visit all outlets on the routes every day.

This July, the company noticed a higher than normal absenteeism on Fridays and Mondays. The drivers call in sick. This has meant that the route supervisors have had to drive the routes themselves. Since many drivers have exceeded their allowable sick days, the company is docking the drivers (i.e., not paying them) for absent days. But this has not reduced the absenteeism.

(a) **Three Minutes** In the space below, list all the reasonable explanations you can think of as to why the drivers are calling in sick on Mondays and Fridays. **Start timing now.**

(b) **Three Minutes** Assuming the explanations you just listed are valid, use the space below to list all the possible actions the bottling company might take to correct the problem. **Start timing now.**

3. **Three Minutes** A friend of yours manufactures peanut butter and other peanut products. Peanut shells are a by-product, and your friend has been carting them to the dump for use as landfill; they are, of course, biodegradable.

You're convinced that the shells will have some commercial value if ways can be found to use them and not merely bury them. In the space below, list all the possible uses that you feel should be explored for their practicality. **Start timing now.**

4. **Three Minutes** Many fruits find their names used in figures of speech. For example, we refer to an unreliable automobile as a "lemon," or the boss or lead performer as the "top banana." In the space below, list all the figures of speech you can think of that have the name of a fruit in them. **Start timing now.**

5. **Three Minutes** It's scrabble time. Here are your seven letters. In the space below, see how many words you can assemble by using some of these letters (and no other letters). A letter may be used only once in each word. **Start timing now.**

NXEYOTI

Fifteen Minutes Complete as many of these assignments as you possibly can. Don't spend too much time on any that stump you. Move on to another. You can always return to an item if a new strategy or fresh insight comes to you. The exercise continues on the next page. **Start timing now.**

6. Describe how you could cut this piece of cheese into eight equal pieces with only three cuts. Answer: _____ _____ _____ _____	7. Join the nine dots shown at the right by drawing four straight lines without lifting your pencil from the paper. Then do the same for the nine dots shown below by drawing three straight lines without lifting your pencil.
8. By drawing one line, convert this odd number into an even number. ## IX	9. You have a 5-minute hourglass and a 3-minute hourglass. You want to measure 7 minutes. How? Answer: _____ _____

10. How many squares are there in this figure?

1	5	9	13
2	6	10	14
3	7	11	15
4	8	12	16

Answer: _____

11. What do the following words have in common?

canopy, deft, first, laughing, hijack, stupid, calmness, labcoat

Answer: _____

_____

_____

12. Add lines to the two identical figures at the right to convert them into three-letter abbreviations for two world-famous organizations.

These organizations are:_____

_____

_____

13. Nine wolves are in this square enclosure at the zoo. Draw two more square enclosures that will put each wolf in a pen by itself.

14. What is the logic behind this sequence of the numbers one through nine?

8, 5, 4, 9, 1, 7, 6, 3, 2

Answer:_____

_____

_____

15.

Three cans are full and three are empty. By moving only one can, see if you can end up with full and empty cans alternating.

Answer: _____

_____

_____

TEST OF CREATIVITY

Answer Sheet and Feedback

The test you just completed covers the major types of mental activity associated with creativity: insight, recognizing relationships that are not easily evident, visualizing, thinking laterally as well as linearly, withholding evaluation (judgment) so as to generate many ideas (brainstorming), using familiar concepts or objects in unfamiliar (novel) ways, and so on.

Creative people tend to have traits that are not shared by most other people. Often they have grown up as "loners," seeking solitude rather than friends and peer group support. They see no reason to conform and meet arbitrary norms. They value their uniqueness and originality. They are not ashamed of having "off-the-wall" thoughts and do not fear the realization that others will see them as bizarre, foolish, or "out-of-touch." They prefer challenge to routine, and value excitement over predictability and fixedness.

Although creativity requires superior intelligence, a high I.Q. is no guarantee of creativity. In fact, only a small fraction of the intellectually gifted are creative. Besides being novel, the fruits of your creativity must also be appropriate or relevant or satisfying to others (for example, aesthetically pleasing in works of art or music). Otherwise, anyone who smears paint on canvas or pounds on piano keys in novel and bizarre ways would have to be deemed creative (and this could include the entire family of man as well as our primate friends, apes, monkeys, and King Kong!).

1. On this first exercise, your mission was to come up with as many words as you can generate in five minutes that begin with the letter c. Did you plunge right in by listing any word that came to mind? Or did you spend a moment planning your creative journey with questions like these:

   (a) Is it better to work through the alphabet so as to avoid later confusion as to whether you've already used a word (e.g., all "ca . . ." words, followed by all "ce . . ." words, "ch . . ." words, etc.)?

   (b) Is it better to write only one-syllable words, since you can write more of them in three minutes (e.g., can, cow, cut, chip versus circumference, communications, celebrity)?

   (c) Is it acceptable to use different forms of the same word (e.g., cheat, cheater, cheats, cheating), or would that not be very challenging or original? (Remember: creative people prefer challenge and excitement to routine and fixedness.)

   All of these questions are rational and analytical, and draw on the left brain. Creative individuals harness and channel their creativity by planning their approach to a creative assignment with such questions. If you did so, you probably realize that: (a) an alphabetic approach would enable you to generate more words in shorter time, since you are following a system rather than a random process; (b) although one-syllable words can be written more quickly, if you start to pass judgment and edit yourself, your momentum will slow down; (c) if you are highly creative, you're likely to be bored by simply sticking different endings onto a root word. You won't see them as new (original, novel) words, and there won't be much challenge or excitement.

Printed below is a list of c words to show how easy it is to follow these (a), (b), (c) guidelines and to generate words as fast as you can write. Writing at a rate of 30 words per minute, you could come up with about 150 words, as shown in the list below. (No need for your list to resemble ours, of course.) Take a moment to count the total number of words you generated in five minutes. Divide this number by five.

Enter the resulting number in the box at the right (total divided by five)

[ ] **1**

CA   cab, cache, cad, cadmium, cadet, cadaver, cafe, cage, cake, calf, caliber, cam, came, can, cane, cap, caper, cape, capillary, car, carnage, carpet, care, carry carrot, carp, case, cast, castle, caste, cat, catch, cater, cattle, cataract, cave, caveat, cavity

CE   cedar, ceiling, certain, celebrity, celery, cell, celtic, cement, cemetery, censor, census, centennial, century, cent, centimeter

CH   chap, char, chat, chant, chair, chablis, chafing, charge, chastise, chapter, charity, chatterbox, cheap, cheat, cheer, chest, check, chef, chip, chicle, chic, chin, chirp, chit, chisel, chimney, chimp, chive, choke, chow, chock, chore, chose, chunk, chute

CI   cigar, cilia, cinder, circle, circumference, circumvent, cistern, city, civics, civil

CL   clone, claw, clasp, cliff, clique, clump, clip, clown, clutch, clef, clean, clear, cloud, clout

CO   cord, con, (convent, convex, convert, control . . . etc.) corn, cob, cod, coffee, cog, cogitate, coke, cold, color, collate, collide, cop, copper, cope, core, cot, cottage, coddle, cove, covey, cover, cow, cower, coy, coyote, cozy

CR   crap, crate, crash, cranberry, crazy, crest, cream, crisp, criterion, croak, crown, crow, croon, crock, crouton, crud, cruller, crust, cruet, cruel

CU   cub, cuckoo, cuckold, cud, cuddle, cue, cuff, culinary, culprit, cull, cunning, cup, cur, curt, curdle, curfew, curate, cure, cusp, cuss, custard, cut, cute

CY   cymbal, cyst, cynic, cycle, cyclical

2. In this exercise, you generated possible explanations in response to (a), then came up with possible solutions in response to (b). We've listed twelve relevant answers to each. Your responses will differ from ours, of course. See how many plausible responses you came up with.

Enter your total to parts (a) and (b) in the box at the right.

	2

(a) • it's summer and they value their three- to four-day weekends more than the money

   • they really are sick, having exerted themselves excessively over the weekend

   • they have Monday hangovers

   • they are paid so well that the docking doesn't hurt them

   • the Friday deliveries are heavier: more work stocking stores for the weekend

   • the Monday "out-of-stocks" (it's summer) mean more work and second trips

   • the routes are too big, too many outlets

   • the traffic on Friday and Monday is too much of a hassle

   • weekend sporting events (stadium, arena, coliseum) require much more labor

   • their trucks can't carry enough product for extra-heavy Monday/Friday deliveries

   • their jobs aren't satisfying; long weekends are providing the balance

   • drivers may be going off in groups for long weekends (hunting, fishing, drinking)

(b) • provide weekend deliveries for stores that have had "out-of-stock" conditions

   • take advance orders by phone so trucks carry only what they need

   • reduce the number and variety of packages (sizes, cans vs. bottles)

   • hire helpers to work with drivers; they can run routes if necessary

   • have retirees on call in case regulars don't show up

   • carry more product: use larger trucks or use pallets for delivery to larger stores

   • increase the penalty for absenteeism

   • reapportion the territory so as to break up larger (out-of-stock) routes

   • set up a special weekend "hot line" so that dealers can phone for supplementary delivery

   • terminate for excessive absenteeism, replace with drivers with a different work ethic

   • deliver product to sporting events during midweek, not on Friday

   • carry only the best sellers on Monday and Friday (80% of sales come from 20% of product line)

3. Creativity requires superior intelligence. In this exercise, you could channel your thinking into a variety of different fields: agriculture, construction, manufacture, and so on. Your ability to "shift gears" and move your focus from one context to another is important to success on exercises such as this.

First of all, you should recognize that peanut shells can be used "as is" in some applications. However, by processing them, we can greatly expand our list of potential uses, as shown in the list below. We've listed 15 applications—many more than you had time to generate or write in 3 minutes.

Enter your total in the box at the right.

☐ **3**

Use peanut shells "as is" for:

- animal feed (silage)

- filler in human food (like soybeans)

- aggregate (additive) in cement for use as stucco—makes it lighter

- fiber in "scratch coat" (undercoat) prior to fine plaster coat

- fiber in asphalt as paving

- pulp to be rolled into special kinds of paper or sheet products

- insulation (if fireproofing is economical or unnecessary)

- additive in potting soil—helps it breathe

- filler in a contained jumping, rolling, bouncing area for children

- filler (sterilized) in pillows, quilts, blankets (like Kapok)

Process the shells (shred, grind, pulverize) to use as:

- mulch and ground cover for planting areas

- fuel, either alone or as additive

- packing material (like styrofoam pellets and squiggles)

- crushable filler in highway and vehicle collision barriers (in bags or plastic canisters)

- additive to plastic, resins, plaster, cement (fibers add strength)

4. If English is not your native language, you will find an exercise like this to be especially challenging. Let's see how the fruits of your labor compare with ours. Listed below are some candidates for "fruity" figures of speech.

Enter your total in the box at the right.

☐ **4**

grapes of wrath	they gave him the raspberry	a blueberry sky
sour grapes	life is a bowl of cherries	that soldier is a cherry
that car is a lemon	turn lemons into lemonade	the apple of her daddy's eye
his new job is a plum	a banana republic	heard it through the grapevine
a peach of a deal	apple polishing is brownnosing	the pineapple failed to detonate
a strawberry blonde	he's a real slick apple	the crowd went bananas
a hot tomato	a strawberry mark on her thigh	he painted it lime (orange, plum)

5. Words formed from these letters are listed below. Note the flow, or sequence, in which the mind can be mapped to go from each word to the next. This helps in identifying the full range of possibilities, or as many as 3 minutes will allow.

NXEYOTI

Enter your total in the box at the right.

☐ **5**

ONYX	TEX	YET	TONE	ON	EN	ONE	TEN
EXIT	NIX	YIN	NOTE	NO	ET	EON	TOE
OX	NEXT	YON	NOT	TO	IT	TIE	TOY
OXEN	NET	TON	NIT	YO	TI	TIN	TONY

---

6. Cut the cheese horizontally into two equal cakes. Then cut vertically into four equal 90° wedges.

7. You must go outside the area of the nine dots to solve each puzzle.

8.

SIX

One line will convert a Roman number nine into a six.

9. Start both glasses simultaneously. When the three runs out, two minutes will remain on the five-minute timer. As soon as the two minutes run out, turn the glass over.

2 + 5 = 7

---

10. 16 individual squares
    4 corner quadrants (e.g., 1, 2, 5, 6)
    1 middle square (6, 7, 10, 11)
    4 arms of a cross (e.g., 2, 3, 6, 7)
    4 corners 3x3 (e.g., 1,2,3, 5,6,7, 9,10,11)
    <u>1</u> biggest square (4x4 squares)
    30

11. Each of these words contains three successive letters of the alphabet:
    nop in canopy, def in deft, rst in first, etc.

12. *USA*   *USN*

United States
of America, or
U.S. Army

United States
Navy

13.

14. Their names are in alphabetic order:

    Eight, Five, Four, Nine, One, Seven, Six, Three, Two

15. Pour the contents of the middle full bucket into the middle empty bucket.

Give yourself two points for each of the ten assignments that you got right. Give one point for half-right answers. The total possible is 20 points.

Enter your total in the box at the right.

6–15

HOW DID YOU DO?

Highly creative persons will usually score in the range of 15–20 points in each of the six boxes, for a total of 90–120 points. Moderately creative persons typically score in the range of 10–15 points on each item, for a total of 60–90 points. Add up your scores in the six boxes, and enter this new total in the box at the right.

What insights have you gained into the nature of creativity and your areas of creative strength and weakness?

❖ Leadership And Team Building ❖

This self-assessment exercise enables a team member or the team leader to review their overall effectiveness by focusing on a number of factors that are important to the success of work groups. There are sixty statements on the pages that follow. Your job is to indicate the extent to which you agree or disagree with each statement, entering the reply on the separate Answer Sheet on page 12 and 13.

Some of the statements will be characteristic of your work team. Others will not be. Your job is to place a circle on the Answer Sheet in the box that best reflects your own opinion of each statement.

- If you <u>definitely agree</u>, place a circle around the two plus signs.
- If you are <u>inclined to agree</u>, place a circle around the one plus sign.
- If you are <u>inclined to disagree</u>, place a circle around the one minus sign.
- If you <u>definitely disagree</u>, place a circle around the two minus signs.

Here is an example:

Personal rivalries are fairly common around here.

Notice that in the sample item above, there is a circle around the box that indicates that the person responding is inclined to agree. As you go through this list of 60 items, place a circle in one of the four boxes for the corresponding number on your answer sheet for each item. You won't know the answer, since the items are statements of opinion rather than factual statements. In other words, your responses will simply indicate the extent to which you agree or disagree with the opinion expressed. Incidentally, you want to be careful that you are placing a circle around the box whose number corresponds to the statement that you are answering at the time.

After completing the exercise, you will be given instructions on how to score your responses and interpret the results. You may want to invite other members of your team (work group, department, branch, etc.) to go through the exercise, in which case you may make copies of the Answer Sheet. By comparing your responses with those of other members of your team and arriving at a composite score or average for the group, you will be able to identify the team's strengths and the areas where your effectiveness is being blocked. This should lead to a discussion by members and leader as to what actions can be taken to improve the team's overall effectiveness.

1. The leader usually discusses issues with the team, and gets their opinions before making decisions. ++ | + | – | – –

2. Sometimes our work suffers because one or more team members lack the ability to handle the situation. ++ | + | – | – –

3. Our members are well committed to the purpose and objectives of the team. ++ | + | – | – –

4. The team needs to spend more time clearing the air of suspicion and distrust among certain members. ++ | + | – | – –

5. The organization does not make intelligent use of our firm's talent. ++ | + | – | – –

6. Our team meetings are productive and we get a lot accomplished. ++ | + | – | – –

7. Some of our people don't know how their own roles relate to the jobs of other team members. ++ | + | – | – –

8. Being a member of our team provides me with a great deal of satisfaction. ++ | + | – | – –

9. We receive frequent and specific feedback of our work. ++ | + | – | – –

10. Our team lacks a good program for developing its members. ++ | + | – | – –

11. The leader is not flexible enough and does not easily adapt to changing circumstances. ++ | + | – | – –

12. Some members are not adapting to the needs of others or to the goals of the team. ++ | + | – | – –

13. In practice, the team often falls short of its objectives. ++ | + | – | – –

14. Our team members are good at working out interpersonal problems and in dealing with one another in openness and candor. ++ | + | – | – –

15. Our team's objectives have not been integrated into the objectives of the entire organization. ++ | + | – | – –

16. At our team meetings, decisions we reach and plans we agree to are often not followed up or acted upon. ++ | + | – | – –

17. We have regular reviews of individual and group objectives. ++ | + | – | – –

18. There are other teams here at work that would be more satisfying to belong to. ++ | + | – | – –

19. Our team members learn well from mistakes and from feedback we get from others. ++ | + | – | – –

20. Our team members have many opportunities for growth and expansion of their skills and knowledge. ++ | + | – | – –

21. Team members do not know where they stand with the leader. ++ | + | – | – –

22. Our team spends a lot of time and energy getting the right members and developing them effectively. ++ | + | – | – –

23. Members have a good record of stretching and knocking themselves out to accomplish the team's mission. ++ | + | – | – –

24. Our team members haven't really gotten to know one another very well as individuals. ++ | + | – | – –

25. Our team works with a clear mission that is known to members and outsiders alike. ++ | + | – | – –

26. Our team members lack a methodical approach to working together in meetings. ++ | + | – | – –

27. We have a long way to go to improve communication between and among team members. ++ | + | – | – –

28. Some of our members are not very satisfied with the way things are going for our team. ++ | + | – | – –

29. We presently lack the ability to review our effectiveness in a constructive, objective manner. ++ | + | – | – –

30. Little time and effort is spent on individual development and training. ++ | + | – | – –

31. The leader welcomes leadership efforts by other team members and encourages initiative. `++` `+` `-` `--`	41. The leader has done a good job of working with members to clarify their expectations and needs. `++` `+` `-` `--`	51. The leader is not sensitive enough to the team's perceptions and ideas. `++` `+` `-` `--`
32. The mix of skills and abilities among our members is very well suited to producing high levels of performance. `++` `+` `-` `--`	42. Sometimes our team is viewed by outsiders as unqualified or inadequate. `++` `+` `-` `--`	52. Our team members are all good at handling their jobs. `++` `+` `-` `--`
33. A lot of energy is absorbed in doing things that do not move us toward our team objectives. `++` `+` `-` `--`	43. Team members rarely let personal interests interfere with the work of the group. `++` `+` `-` `--`	53. Some members do not have a strong sense of belonging to the team or identifying with its goals. `++` `+` `-` `--`
34. Our group tends to be frank and open, with members telling each other just how they feel. `++` `+` `-` `--`	44. Internal backbiting, politics, and cliques sometimes interfere with the team's effectiveness. `++` `+` `-` `--`	54. We relate well as group members and have developed a healthy level of trust and openness. `++` `+` `-` `--`
35. If our team were dissolved, the organization would experience a substantial loss. `++` `+` `-` `--`	45. There is confusion between our team's work and the work of others. `++` `+` `-` `--`	55. Our team's contribution is understood and respected by others with whom we work. `++` `+` `-` `--`
36. We are pretty good at using team meetings to resolve conflicts, solve problems, and build commitment. `++` `+` `-` `--`	46. I don't see much benefit from the team meetings I've attended. `++` `+` `-` `--`	56. We use our time effectively when we get together; very little time is wasted. `++` `+` `-` `--`
37. Our team members have a good understanding of how to use one another and the resources of the organization. `++` `+` `-` `--`	47. Our interpersonal relations among team members need improvement. `++` `+` `-` `--`	57. We relate well to one another and have developed fairly effective ways of working together. `++` `+` `-` `--`
38. I am proud to be a member of our work team. `++` `+` `-` `--`	48. Morale on our team is not what it should be. `++` `+` `-` `--`	58. Sometimes we fail to appreciate the many benefits of being a member of our team. `++` `+` `-` `--`
39. We do a good job of reviewing the team's performance and what we as individuals can do to improve it. `++` `+` `-` `--`	49. We tend to avoid feedback and critiques. `++` `+` `-` `--`	59. Our reviews of team performance tend to rock the boat and end up jeopardizing our working relationships. `++` `+` `-` `--`
40. Our team members have shown good initiative in developing themselves. `++` `+` `-` `--`	50. Many team members have had almost no individual development beyond their area of specialty. `++` `+` `-` `--`	60. We've done a good job of training and developing our team members. `++` `+` `-` `--`

Leadership And Team Building

Answer Sheet

Directions: Add up the six circled scores that appear side by side across the page. Be sure that you are adding horizontally (sideways), rather than in the usual vertical manner. The sum of these six scores reflects your views of your team's **Leadership.** Enter the sum in the box to the right of the **Leadership** scores.

Now do the same for each of the other nine horizontal groupings. Each score that you enter will be the sum of six circled numbers. The highest score possible is a 24; the lowest is a 6.

Don't worry about what the scores mean. You'll be discussing the interpretations after everyone has completed the scoring.

1. | 4 | 3 | 2 | 1 | 11. | 4 | 3 | 2 | 1 | 21. | 4 | 3 | 2 | 1 | 31. | 4 | 3 | 2 | 1 | 41. | 4 | 3 | 2 | 1 | 51. | 4 | 3 | 2 | 1 |
LEADERSHIP, or the appropriateness of the supervision that the team receives... ☐

2. | 4 | 3 | 2 | 1 | 12. | 4 | 3 | 2 | 1 | 22. | 4 | 3 | 2 | 1 | 32. | 4 | 3 | 2 | 1 | 42. | 4 | 3 | 2 | 1 | 52. | 4 | 3 | 2 | 1 |
MEMBERSHIP, or having persons with the right qualifications on the team... ☐

3. | 4 | 3 | 2 | 1 | 13. | 4 | 3 | 2 | 1 | 23. | 4 | 3 | 2 | 1 | 33. | 4 | 3 | 2 | 1 | 43. | 4 | 3 | 2 | 1 | 53. | 4 | 3 | 2 | 1 |
COMMITMENT, or a sense of belonging to and identifying with the team .... ☐

4. | 4 | 3 | 2 | 1 | 14. | 4 | 3 | 2 | 1 | 24. | 4 | 3 | 2 | 1 | 34. | 4 | 3 | 2 | 1 | 44. | 4 | 3 | 2 | 1 | 54. | 4 | 3 | 2 | 1 |
TRUST/OPENNESS, or a climate of relaxed, frank, open communications .... ☐

5. | 4 | 3 | 2 | 1 | 15. | 4 | 3 | 2 | 1 | 25. | 4 | 3 | 2 | 1 | 35. | 4 | 3 | 2 | 1 | 45. | 4 | 3 | 2 | 1 | 55. | 4 | 3 | 2 | 1 |
MISSION, or clarity of team's role and identity in the larger organization... ☐

6. | 4 | 3 | 2 | 1 | 16. | 4 | 3 | 2 | 1 | 26. | 4 | 3 | 2 | 1 | 36. | 4 | 3 | 2 | 1 | 46. | 4 | 3 | 2 | 1 | 56. | 4 | 3 | 2 | 1 |
MEETINGS, or productiveness of the team when members meet as a group... ☐

7. | 4 | 3 | 2 | 1 | 17. | 4 | 3 | 2 | 1 | 27. | 4 | 3 | 2 | 1 | 37 | 4 | 3 | 2 | 1 | 47. | 4 | 3 | 2 | 1 | 57. | 4 | 3 | 2 | 1 |
RELATIONSHIPS, or how well members work together and relate to one another... ☐

8. | 4 | 3 | 2 | 1 | 18. | 4 | 3 | 2 | 1 | 28. | 4 | 3 | 2 | 1 | 38. | 4 | 3 | 2 | 1 | 48. | 4 | 3 | 2 | 1 | 58. | 4 | 3 | 2 | 1 |
SATISFACTION, or the personal rewards that come from belonging to the team... ☐

9. | 4 | 3 | 2 | 1 | 19. | 4 | 3 | 2 | 1 | 29. | 4 | 3 | 2 | 1 | 319 | 4 | 3 | 2 | 1 | 49. | 4 | 3 | 2 | 1 | 59. | 4 | 3 | 2 | 1 |
FEEDBACK, or the degree to which the group reviews its performance .... ☐

10. | 4 | 3 | 2 | 1 | 20. | 4 | 3 | 2 | 1 | 30. | 4 | 3 | 2 | 1 | 40. | 4 | 3 | 2 | 1 | 50. | 4 | 3 | 2 | 1 | 60. | 4 | 3 | 2 | 1 |
DEVELOPMENT, or the opportunities for growth and further training.. ☐

Leadership And Team Building

Interpretation

Directions: Take each of the ten sums from the prior page and convert it to a rank, as shown. Then enter the ranks in the boxes to the left.

1. **Performing appropriate leadership roles**—The leader discusses issues and gets facts and opinions before decisions are made. Team members know where they stand with the leader, who gives feedback to members. The leader encourages initiative and welcomes leadership efforts by other team members.

Raw Scores	Rank
23, 24	10
21, 22	9
19, 20	8
17, 18	7
15, 16	6
13, 14	5
11, 12	4
9, 10	3
8	2
7	1
6	0

2. **Having the right members**—The team members possess a mix of skills and abilities needed to produce high levels of performance. They are good at handling their jobs and are viewed by outsiders as qualified. Members adapt to the needs of others or to the goals of the team. A lot of time is spent getting the right members and developing them effectively.

3. **Winning the commitment of members**—Members have a strong sense of belonging to the team and identifying with its goals. Objectives are met since members knock themselves out to accomplish their goals. Team activities are carefully planned to move the team toward meeting objectives without wasting time and energy.

4. **Building a climate of trust and openness**—A healthy level of trust and openness exists among team members. When interpersonal problems arise, they are dealt with candidly and honestly before they are allowed to disrupt the positive climate. Internal backbiting, politics, and cliques do not interfere with the team's effectiveness.

5. **Clarifying the mission**—The organization understands and respects contributions made by the team and would experience a substantial loss if the team did not exist. The mission of the team is known to members and non-members alike. The objectives of the team are integrated into the objectives of the entire organization.

6. **Using meetings to build teamwork**—The time spent at meetings is used effectively in resolving conflicts, solving problems, and building commitment. The decisions reached and plans made are followed up and acted upon by members. Meetings are run using a methodical approach understood and supported by team members.

7. **Developing relationships**—Team members have developed fairly effective ways of working together and know how to use one another as resources. Members know how their roles relate to the roles and responsibilities of other team members. As the team develops, interpersonal relations among members are improved and strengthened.

8. **Cultivating job satisfaction**—Members experience a great deal of satisfaction and pride in being part of the team and do not choose to belong to another team. Being a member of the team means receiving psychological (intrinsic) and financial (extrinsic) rewards. Team morale is high and stays that way even when problems arise.

9. **Improving the quality of feedback**—The team views mistakes as learning experiences. Team performance is reviewed in a constructive and objective manner. Members give and receive feedback and suggest how to improve team performance. Reviews of team performance do not end up jeopardizing working relationships among members.

10. **Training and developing the team**—Team members have many opportunities for growth and enlargement of their skills and abilities within and beyond their individual areas of specialty. Members initiate self-development programs to benefit team performance.

Now add the numbers in the preceding ten boxes. A "perfect" score is 100. How well did your own team score? A score of 70 or less indicates that there is room for improvement. More important, you know which items to concentrate on—those with the lowest scores.

Building a Winning Team

One way of looking at the elements of a successful team-building effort is to examine the similarities between work teams and sports teams. Developing an effective work team is not too different from developing a winning sports team.

To begin with, the leader relates to team members as one adult to another. Members are individuals who bring their own needs and interests to the game, and the leader helps them clarify their needs and expectations. Each member of a team must contribute his/her own particular skills and expertise. On a football team, the skills needed to be a good tackler are quite different from those needed to be a good kicker or passer. However, for the team to be successful, it needs everyone's skills. A team made up of all passers won't be a winning team. In short, teams need members with a variety of different skills.

Likewise, a successful work team needs members who bring to the group their own specific knowledge and skills. A work team designed to explore ways of increasing productivity will need the perspective of a manager as well as a production worker. Each member makes a different yet significant contribution to the team as a whole. In this way, members not only gain an appreciation for the different dimensions of the organization, but the team as a unit also benefits from a broad-based perspective on any single issue.

In sports and at work, players share a common goal: they want to belong to a winning team. No one wants to be in last place at the end of the season. Members come together to work on a specific project, and each has a stake in the outcome. Members want to work as an effective team and to complete their tasks successfully. They are united by their shared desire to achieve a common goal.

Players come to the realization that they are interdependent. The quarterback or the coach cannot win the game without the talents and support of all the other players. This applies to work teams as well. There are no "stars" in work teams . . . only "star" teams.

As each team member learns about each other's skills and ability, trust and respect begin to develop. This positive climate fuels feelings of togetherness among team members. When a player and a coach don't get along, the positive climate of the whole team is threatened, since players may begin to take sides with one or the other. A work team containing one member who is an excessive talker or is aggressive may have a difficult time maintaining a supportive climate.

Both sports teams and work teams use methods that keep the ball moving. Football teams rely on offensive and defensive play-selection, signal-calling, and follow-through. And they have post-game critiques and pre-game planning sessions. Work teams also meet to assess performance, tackle problems, and make decisions. They use techniques such as brainstorming, consensus, problem analysis, and problem solving during their meetings. Many of these same techniques are used on the job when time permits.

A sports team receives immediate feedback for each play. The crowd cheers, and the coach and team members congratulate each other. If the play is unsuccessful, the cheers give way to groans, and on Monday morning the coach reviews the game with the team in order to point out errors. The feedback for a successful work team may not be as dramatic as it is for a sports team. Even if the team has not achieved its goal, the team must evaluate itself on a regular basis and carry out changes whenever needed. Team members can—and should—appraise each other's performance without threatening the positive climate.

Teams and Traditional Work Units: Some Differences

FACTOR	TEAMS	TRADITIONAL WORK UNITS
Nature of Goals	Goals are immediate, common, and foremost in the thinking of every member. The team's acceptance by others depends on achieving these goals.	Goals are longer range, not always common to all, and thought about from time to time. There is a tendency to be task-oriented rather than goal-oriented.
Dependency of Workers	Members depend on each other to achieve goals. They appraise one another's performance, and help one another develop.	Workers depend on a supervisor to give assignments, appraise performance, and provide development.
Visibility and Feedback	Everyone knows very quickly how everyone else is doing. There is high visibility and immediate feedback from peers, from the coach, and from those affected by the team's performance.	An individual can perform well or poorly for days and sometimes even weeks without being recognized. Feedback is sparse and often occurs too late to be of help in shaping performance.
Performance Standards	Extremely high standards and expectations are usually set and measured by the team.	Standards are either nonexistent or are set by the supervisor.
Competition	Each member is trying to beat his or her own last performance. Competition is fair and is not directed toward each other.	Where competition exists, it is between workers and may thus be unfair (since they may not have an equal chance at succeeding).
Morale	Great "esprit de corps" and feeling of privilege in belonging to the team. Others want to belong but are not qualified.	Can vary from very healthy to sick. Usually no particular distinction is attached to belonging to the unit.
Role of Leader	Leader is a coach whose only job is to develop a winning team. The coach does not play the game.	Leader has his or her own work to do, often leaving relatively little time to develop workers.

Some Implications

1. The team you just evaluated is strongest on the following two to three characteristics:

2. The areas that need to be strengthened are (name two to three):

3. Do you feel that your total score is an accurate reflection of how your group functions as a team? _____ Explain:

4. Some of the actions the team might take in order to improve in the areas just noted:

5. Some of the actions you as an individual might take to improve the team:

6. Would it help if other members of the team were to go through this assessment so that you could share your perceptions and discuss possible actions? _____
   If yes, decide who should take the assessment and when you will talk with them.

PART 3
The Culture of Innovation

❖ Determine Your Current Culture ❖

SURVEY OF ATTITUDES TOWARD WORK

In the exercise printed on the next two pages, you will be given a series of 24 statements and asked to indicate your agreement or disagreement with each. To the right of each statement, you will find four boxes.

- If you strongly agree, place an X on the two plus signs.

- If you agree somewhat, place an X on the one plus sign.

- If you disagree somewhat, place an X on the one minus sign.

- If you strongly disagree, place an X on the two minus signs.

The statements you are responding to are statements of opinion. There is no correct answer. Thus, your response should indicate the way you feel rather than what you think the best answer is. In other words, select the box that conveys the extent of your agreement or disagreement with each statement. Answer all statements.

Here's an example. Consider the statement below:

1. Most managers are interested only in productivity and output, and are not really concerned with the feelings of employees.

The person who completed the statement above strongly disagreed with it, as indicated by the X placed in the last box.

Now go through the survey. You will find scoring instructions on the page that follows the 24 statements.

1. Most employees feel that it's pretty important to keep management happy and stay in the boss' good favor. `++` `+` `−` `− −`

2. The typical employee has a wealth of talent and energy that is just waiting to be challenged and channeled. `++` `+` `−` `− −`

3. Policies and procedures are very important, since employees need to know exactly what they can and can't do, and what the penalties are when the rules are broken. `++` `+` `−` `− −`

4. Employees usually want to turn in the best performance they can, and will willingly take on more responsibility or extra work if they understand why it's important. `++` `+` `−` `− −`

5. Workers depend heavily on the company and the boss for their well-being; it is important that the boss like them. `++` `+` `−` `− −`

6. If companies treated their workers as responsible adults rather than as immature children, they would get better performance and the work would be more pleasant. `++` `+` `−` `− −`

7. In most organizations, the employees need to be watched and given close supervision to make sure that the work is done correctly and on time. `++` `+` `−` `− −`

8. Employees like to know what management is thinking and doing in all aspects of the organization, not just in their own department. `++` `+` `−` `− −`

9. Today's employees seem to lack commitment and loyalty to the very company that pays them and provides their benefits. `++` `+` `−` `− −`

10. The majority of workers will think and act responsibly and will turn in good performance once they know the goals and are given regular feedback on how they are doing. `++` `+` `−` `− −`

11. Strong disciplinary measures are essential, since there are a number of employees who will get away with all they can and for whom verbal reprimands are not enough. `++` `+` `−` `− −`

12. The goal of any organization should be to have each employee managing his/her own work without close supervision. `++` `+` `−` `− −`

13. Employees are typically unable to set goals and standards governing their output; management must do so for them. `++ | + | – | – –`

14. Companies make a mistake by not getting their employees more involved in making management decisions. `++ | + | – | – –`

15. Employees are generally more interested in whether the boss likes them than they are in getting specific feedback on the quality of their work. `++ | + | – | – –`

16. Once employees know the goals and standards of their work unit, they can work out the details of how the work can best be done. `++ | + | – | – –`

17. Most workers need a boss who is something of a father and mother to them, sometimes praising, sometimes scolding, and always watching them and taking care of them. `++ | + | – | – –`

18. Most employees want to do more than simply please the boss; they want to meet goals and standards and achieve something. `++ | + | – | – –`

19. Despite the raises and good performance ratings that are given out from time to time, the majority of workers are turning in deficient performance, and their supervisors often know it. `++ | + | – | – –`

20. Managers who expect more from their workers usually get more, while managers who expect less usually get less. `++ | + | – | – –`

21. Even though books about management stress the importance of delegating and "getting work done through others," it is often necessary for supervisors to step in and do the work themselves when a subordinate has failed to do so. `++ | + | – | – –`

22. Once they are sure the goals are understood, managers should give their employees a wide latitude of freedom in meeting them. `++ | + | – | – –`

23. The two things employees want most are pay and a happy boss. `++ | + | – | – –`

24. Employees want to be told when they have succeeded and failed, and want a boss who gives regular and specific feedback. `++ | + | – | – –`

SURVEY OF ATTITUDES TOWARD WORK

SCORING INSTRUCTIONS

Now you are ready to score yourself. Follow these instructions:

- Under each box that contains an X, place the number 3, 2, 1, or 0 to indicate its value. The value of each X is as follows:

3	2	1	0

- Thus, if your X was on the single plus sign, you will enter a 2 under that box, as shown.

++	⊠	-	--

2

- Add up your scores for items 1, 3, 5, 7, 9, 11, 13, 15, 17, 19, 21, and 23 (that is, the odd-numbered items). Enter this total in the box at the right.

(parent-child)

- Now add up your scores for items 2, 4, 6, 8, 10, 12, 14, 16, 18, 20, 22, and 24 (that is, the even-numbered items). Enter this total in the box at the right.

(adult-adult)

The highest score possible in each box is 36, while the lowest score possible is a 0. Each score reflects the relative strength of two different views of work, the "parent-child" view and the "adult-adult" view. We are all a combination of both views. Which is your stronger view? Under what conditions are your views "parent-child"? When are they "adult-adult"?

The "parent-child" view of work:	The "adult-adult" view of work:
Workers are basically children, dependent on management to fill a parent role (making all the decisions and assignments, watching closely to see that workers do what they are supposed to, and giving praise or correction). Workers don't want to make decisions, set goals, evaluate their own performance, manage time effectively, etc. They are content to put in their time playing with the other children. Management must thus tell them what to do and how to do it, and must set up rewards for good performance and punishment (discipline) for non-compliance.	Workers and managers are adults. They share the same human needs, interests, and goals. Most workers want a say in how the work is done and how performance can be improved. Workers want to grow and take on more responsibility. They come to a new job hoping to be challenged. A major goal of the organization is to have every employee function as his/her own manager, making responsible decisions and turning in high performance with a minimum of supervision. Managers who treat workers as equals (fellow adults) will expect more from them and will usually get it. This requires continuous feedback from the manager.

❖ Open Source Innovation ❖

🕐 *2 hours*

Purpose　　The purpose of this exercise is to give participants an opportunity to craft an open source innovation strategy.

Materials
- ✓ Flipchart paper
- ✓ Markers
- ✓ Laptop computers with Internet access (optional)
- ✓ Not invented here—Not

Procedure

1. Ask the participants to define "open source innovation." Simply put, it is the process of obtaining innovative ideas from many sources, including from people outside your organization. You might mention that the packaged goods company Proctor and Gamble made it a corporate goal to raise the number of innovative products *developed on the outside* from about 10% to 50%. A related concept is "crowd sourcing." Crowd sourcing is open sourcing using social network tools.

2. Divide the larger group into smaller groups of 3–7 participants and tell the groups that they will be competing with each other in a contest. Tell the groups that their task is to create a high-powered open source innovation contest for a client. The winner will be the group deemed most likely to acquire the most high-quality ideas.

3. To create these contests, the groups should:

   a) Choose a client organization. It should be an organization with which the group members are familiar: a church, Walmart, Walgreens, a sports team, a food shelf, a restaurant, a city, a political party.

   b) Choose an organizational goal or a problem that needs to be solved. Examples might include the following:
   - a church's goal to increase membership
   - a city's plan for a newly acquired vacant lot
   - new product offerings for a company
   - food shelf's drive for new volunteers or donations
   - a minor league baseball team's goal to make their games more exciting
   - a college's goal to increase enrollment

4. **Note:** Groups can *either* garner ideas to solve the problem *or* try to solve the problem. It is up to the group.

5. Each group needs to distill their idea on to one flip chart page. They will present the idea (in less than five minutes) to the larger group. The members of the larger group can ask clarifying questions.

6. After all groups have presented their ideas, each member of the larger group gets to vote on the plan most likely to succeed. Each participant will place a Post-it Note on the plan that they think is best.

Debrief   Start with a large group discussion on the various open source ideas. What makes for a strong open source campaign? What elements reward participants? What might pique the interest of uninterested people? The larger question is, "How do you enlarge the community that is interested in your endeavors?"

If the group has Internet access, you should suggest that they call up "My Starbucks Idea" (Starbuck's successful open source sight) or General Electric's "Ecomagination Challenge" (General Electric's open source effort at creating energy-saving projects).

❖ Killing the Naysayer ❖

⏱ *30 minutes*

Purpose   The purpose of this exercise is to expose idea-killing phrases and learn how to deal with them.

Materials
- ✓ Flipchart paper
- ✓ Markers
- ✓ Notebook paper
- ✓ Sense of humor
- ✓ Imaginary machete

Procedure
1. Divide the larger group into smaller groups.

2. Ask each group to brainstorm phrases that kill ideas that they hear in their organization. Examples might include:
   - That would not work here.
   - We tried that five years ago.
   - Top management will never go for that.
   - It is not our job to come up with new products.
   - We can never afford something like that.

3. After 5 to 10 minutes, have each group present some of their phrases to the larger group.

4. Have the smaller groups reconvene. Ask them to develop one or two "comebacks" for each of the killer phrases. These should be appropriate and effective comebacks, not just insults or put-downs.

5. Have each group present the "comebacks" to the larger group.

Debrief   This exercise can lead to the larger topics of organizational impediments to change and innovation. It may lead to underlying cultural constraints, some of which cannot be removed by the participants. You might want to develop two lists: "cultural constraints we can move" and "cultural constraints that are immutable."

You should not allow this conversation fall into a "complaint" session where the participants feel that the organization is too powerful and entrenched in order to change. You should bring the conversation back to what is possible within the organizational constraints.

❖ Where do babies (innovative ideas) ❖ come from?

🕐 *2 hours (to weeks and months—this could be part of a strategic planning process)*

Purpose   The purpose of this exercise is to push the participants to think about new sources of innovative ideas. Participants will also develop an action plan for capturing those ideas.

Materials
- ✓ Flipchart paper
- ✓ Markers
- ✓ Diligence and persistence
- ✓ Worksheet #13
- ✓ Laptop computers with Internet access (optional)

Procedure
1. Hand out Worksheet #13.

2. As a large group, discuss each of these items and develop a list of examples for each of them. For example:
   a) *Unexpected occurrences:* 9/11, tsunami, oil spill, earthquake
   a) *Incongruities:* high cost of AIDS drugs
   a) *Process needs:* faster, fewer steps, digitalization
   a) *Market and industry changes:* outsourcing, price compression, savvy consumers
   a) *Demographic changes:* aging Baby Boomers, Tech-savvy Millennials
   a) *Changes in perception:* green is gold, thrifty is good
   a) *New inventions:* digital technology, new medicines, electric engines

3. Divide the larger group into smaller groups. Have each small group choose one or two of these "sources of innovation." The groups need to develop an organizational action plan around one or two of these sources. For instance, if they choose "changing demographics," they can choose a subgroup or two and create a mini-marketing plan around a product or service to meet the needs of this group. These product/service offerings should include:
   a) product/service description
   a) promotional strategy, including social media strategy
   a) pricing strategy
   a) distribution strategy
   a) customer service strategy

4. Have the groups present their product/service ideas to the larger group.

Debrief   The point of this exercise is to have participants expand their thinking about the origins of innovations. Ask participants about their process in doing this exercise. The responses might range from frustration to fun. Yes, it is frustrating trying to create an entire product offering in a short time, but you might reinforce that this is just practice in order to get them in the habit of finding innovations.

Worksheet #13
Sources of Innovation

Unexpected occurrences

Incongruities

Process needs

Industry and market changes

Demographic changes

Changes of perception

New knowledge

Innovation at Work: 55 Activities to Spark Your Team's Creativity, Published by AMACOM Books
American Management Association, www.amanet.org.

119

❖ Failure Notebook ❖

🕐 *30 minutes*

Purpose The purpose of this exercise is to begin to create a productive failure/learning book for an organization.

Materials ✓ Ability to laugh at oneself
✓ Laptop computer for each small group

Procedure 1. Tell the larger group that it is time to laugh at ourselves and have fun with it.

2. Divide the larger group into smaller groups of 3–7 participants.

3. Have each group brainstorm mistakes they have made and what they have learned from those mistakes. Limit the brainstorm, if you can, to work-related issues. Others can then understand the contexts of these mistakes.

4. Have a scribe for each group type these in a database or on a PowerPoint.

5. After about 15 minutes, have each group report-out their findings.

6. To make it more fun or funny, take a vote on which was the biggest blunder.

Debrief Tell the larger group how some organizations institutionalize their failures. Have the participants talk about their experiences in this exercise. Did they feel shame or humiliation? Or did it feel good knowing that others made serious errors?

Make the point that if we can learn from our mistakes, we can learn together. If we shared like this often, we would not make the same errors over and over again.

❖ Faces of Innovation ❖

🕐 *30 minutes*

Purpose The purpose of this exercise is to help participants understand that there are different ways of being innovative.

Materials
✓ Worksheet #14
✓ Notebook paper
✓ Pen
✓ Broad working definition of *innovation*

Procedure
1. Divide the larger group into smaller groups of 3 to 7 participants.

2. Hand out Worksheet #14 and let participants read it for a few minutes.

3. Explain to participants that innovation involves many roles and many hats.

4. Ask them to think about which of these ten faces that they play out in the workplace. Have them present these to their small groups. Have them explain how they play these out and which behaviors they exhibit.

5. After all the groups are finished with that part, ask them to think deeply about which roles are missing in their organization. How could they fill those roles? What kinds of people could fill those roles? How could a group, using a disciplined approach, fill those roles?

6. Facilitate a large-group discussion to finish the exercise.

Debrief Diversity is important to the innovation process. A room full of wild-eyed, creative thinkers may not accomplish much. In organizations, different skill sets are necessary to be innovative. In many cases, no role is any more or less important than another role. Discuss each of these faces and how participants might be able to uncover and expand their own and others' innovative techniques within an organization.

Worksheet #14
The Ten Faces of Innovation

The Learning Personas

Anthropologist: observes human beings and develops a deep understanding of how people interact physically and emotionally with products, services, and spaces

Experimenter: prototypes new ideas continually, learning by an enlightened trial and error

Cross-Pollinator: explores other industries and cultures and then translates those findings and revelations to fit the unique needs of your enterprise

The Organizing Personas

Hurdler: knows the path to innovation is strewn with obstacles and develops a knack for overcoming or outsmarting those roadblocks

Collaborator: helps bring eclectic groups together and often leads from the middle of the pack to create new combinations and multidisciplinary solutions

Director: not only gathers together a talented cast and crew but also helps spark their creative talents

The Building Personas

Experienced Architect: designs compelling experiences that go beyond mere functionality to connect at a deeper level with customers' latent or expressed needs

Set Designer: creates a stage on which innovation team members can do their best work, transforming physical environments into powerful tools to influence behavior and attitude

Caregiver: builds on the metaphor of a health care professional to deliver customer care in a manner that goes beyond mere service

Storyteller: builds both internal morale and external awareness through compelling narratives that communicate a fundamental human value or reinforce a specific cultural trait

Innovation at Work: 55 Activities to Spark Your Team's Creativity, Published by AMACOM Books
American Management Association, www.amanet.org.

125

❖ Event/Pattern/Structure ❖

🕐 *60 minutes*

Purpose The purpose of this exercise is to introduce systems thinking as an important part of innovation.

Materials
- ✓ Flipchart paper
- ✓ Markers
- ✓ Wide-angle view of life

Procedure

1. Divide the larger group into smaller groups of 3 to 7 participants.

2. Introduce the concept of event/pattern/structure:
   a) *Event:* actual event occurrence
   b) *Pattern:* series of like events or occurrences
   c) *Structure:* the underlying structure that is creating the pattern

3. Example:
   a) *Event:* a fender-bender car accident at a particular corner
   b) *Pattern:* series of the events or occurrences
   c) *Structure:* the underlying structure that is creating the pattern

4. Ask each group to choose a negative event or occurrence in their workplace. Have them figure out if there is a pattern. (Examples might include chronically late reports, dirty restrooms, or delayed shipments.)

5. Have the groups brainstorm and figure out the underlying structures that are causing these patterns.

6. Have the groups brainstorm (they can use one of the techniques delineated in this book) possible "fixes" for these underlying structural problems.

7. Have the groups report-out their findings to the larger group.

Debrief Systems thinkers think in terms of underlying structures and not just events. It is important to look deeply for the underlying problems, not just surface issues. Otherwise, you might be solving the wrong problem, and the solution will not last.

This author once worked with a second-grade teacher. When a particular little boy acted out inappropriately, she would take away his recess time. Guess what? That just exacerbated the problem. Why? Because he was severely ADHD, taking recess away just made him more fidgety and prone to acting out. A better solution in this case might have been to have him sweep the floor or run files from room to room.

❖ Trend Spotting ❖

🕐 *1–2 hours*

Purpose
The purpose of this exercise is to give participants practice in spotting trends and translating those trends into possible innovations.

Materials
- ✓ Notebook paper
- ✓ Pens
- ✓ Fiery imagination
- ✓ Laptop computers or iPads (one for every two participants)

Procedure
1. Divide the larger group into smaller groups of 4 to 8 participants. Distribute the laptops/iPads.

2. Explain that the purpose of this exercise is to give participants practice in spotting and working with trends in the marketplace.

3. Have each group choose an industry: auto, coffee shop, oil, fashion, craft shops.

4. The first task of the groups is to investigate the industry. They can use Google or another Internet search engine. They could type in "office furniture, innovations."

5. While half the group "surfs," the other half should take notes. What trends, innovations, initiatives, new policies, or events are happening in that industry?

6. After about 20–30 minutes, the groups should switch to an innovation mode. Given these trends and other industry news, what innovations is this industry ready for? What needs are being created by the trends, innovations, and events? Have the groups spend 20 minutes brainstorming possible innovations.

7. Have the smaller groups report-out to the larger group.

Debrief
Innovations spawn other innovations. Initiatives spawn innovations. Events create space for innovations. For instance, cell phones created a billion-dollar ringtone industry. Gas-fueled autos spawned a huge oil-drilling industry.

To get ahead of the curve, individuals and organizations must be constantly monitoring trends and innovations. What is next in that business or industry? You can ask how organizations and individuals can methodically and systematically collect trends and act on them. This will be a rich conversation.

❖ Creative Collaboration ❖

Purpose   The purpose of this exercise is to help participants use concepts of creative collaboration and evaluate their organizations with them.

Materials
- ✓ Flipchart paper
- ✓ Markers
- ✓ Notebook paper
- ✓ Pens
- ✓ Worksheet #15

Procedure   1. Divide the larger group into smaller groups of 4 to 8 participants.

2. Distribute Worksheet #15, which lists principles of creative collaboration.

3. Have each group choose an industry: auto, coffee shop, oil, fashion, craft shops.

4. Discuss the concept of creative collaboration with participants. Creative collaboration is a stepping stone to innovation. The more creative collaboration in a group, the more likely the group is to produce new, productive ideas.

5. Each group should divide a flip chart page in half vertically. They should label each column "Helpful" and "Not Helpful" (to Creative Collaboration). Using the worksheet ideas, they should brainstorm behaviors and attitudes for these two columns.

Debrief   Very little is done in isolation. To tackle complex problems, we clearly need creative collaboration at its best. Everyone in organizations needs to learn how to play well in the sand box.

During this debrief, if a participant says something like "communicate better," ask him or her to go deeper. What exactly do they mean by communication? In what context? Ask participants for specific action steps to make their workplace more conducive to creative collaboration.

Worksheet #15
Principles of Creative Collaboration

Open, advanced communication: Participants should be trained on how to build on to each other's voices and incorporate respectful give and take as part of the creative process.

Diversity of voices: Many different voices help with creative collaboration. People with diverse perspectives see things in differing but interesting and complex ways.

Community space for communication: Nurses use logs. Many new computer programs allow for joint creation of documents or drawings. Bulletin boards allow for messaging during non-meeting times.

Watering holes: Creative collaboration necessitates a place where people can come together naturally, usually around food or coffee. It may be a coffee shop, a table out in the open, or a conference room.

Open time: There needs to be time dedicated to innovation and collaboration. It cannot be an afterthought.

"Yes, and" rather than "yes, but": This is a subtle but powerful distinction. It is an active push to get negative language away from the act of creation.

Rapid prototyping: It does not matter if it is a three-dimensional representation or a sketch on a pad of paper. It is important to create a working prototype in order to have something to which to react.

Innovation at Work: 55 Activities to Spark Your Team's Creativity, Published by AMACOM Books
American Management Association, www.amanet.org.

133

❖ Building an Innovative Culture I ❖

🕐 *30 minutes*

Purpose   The purpose of this exercise is to give participants a start on building an innovative culture in their workplace.

Materials   ✓ Worksheet #16
                ✓ Pens
                ✓ Laptop computer with Internet access (optional)

Procedure   1. Divide the larger group into smaller groups of 4–7 participants.

                2. Distribute Worksheet #16.

                3. Have the groups fill in the worksheets as well as they can. Have them be creative. The goal is to have an action plan for creating an innovative workplace. They might get into a mode of "we cannot do this because..." but help them past this phase. There will always be resistant to new ideas.

                4. Have participants use the computers to look up books or articles that may be useful.

                5. Have participants share their ideas with others in the larger group.

Debrief   Innovation can be fun. Make it so. Build innovation activities into the calendar; do not wait for them to happen on their own. Innovation activities can be high energy. Add food and playfulness to the mix.

                Emphasize that innovation is doable. It does not necessarily take a huge budget, creative geniuses, or expensive retreats to a mountaintop hideout, even though those are nice. Departments can take their own innovation initiatives and make them work. These efforts can become infectious to those around the initiators.

                The important part is to start somewhere, even if it is just a once-a-month, lunch book club.

Worksheet #16
Building an Innovative Culture

INITIATIVE	ACTION #1	ACTION #2	ACTION #3
Innovation Book Club			
Failure Party			
Innovation Story Communication			
Prototype Development Party			
Innovation Room Development			
Trend Spotting Group			
Customer Probing Circle			
Process Redesign Initiative			
Other			

Innovation at Work: 55 Activities to Spark Your Team's Creativity, Published by AMACOM Books
American Management Association, www.amanet.org.

137

❖ Building an Innovative Culture II ❖

Purpose   The purpose of this exercise is to help an organization gauge its openness to innovation.

Materials   ✓ Critical eye
                    ✓ Worksheet #17
                    ✓ Pens

Procedure   1. Divide the larger group into smaller groups of 4 to 7 participants.

                    2. Distribute Worksheet #17.

                    3. Ask participants to look critically at their organization and the checklist. In each category, how does the organization do well, and when does it fall short?

                    4. Have smaller groups report-out their findings to the larger group.

Debrief   What makes for an innovative workplace? Participants can give many deterrents to innovation, but can they conceive and execute a culture that encourages innovation? This exercise allows them to break down parts of a culture and examine it, and to see how to improve it. The biggest takeaway from this exercise can be the conversations that take place.

                    Ask participants which elements are missing and how to bring those forward. Ask them which of those elements on Worksheet #17 are hardest to build into the culture.

Worksheet #17
A Culture of Innovation

Write down two or three examples of each of these elements that are embedded in your culture.

- Open Dialogue

    - _____
    - _____
    - _____

- Encourage New Ideas

    - _____
    - _____
    - _____

- Sufficient Resources

    - _____
    - _____
    - _____

- Reinforcement

    - _____
    - _____
    - _____

- Respect

    - _____
    - _____
    - _____

- Opportunity

    - _____
    - _____
    - _____

Innovation at Work: 55 Activities to Spark Your Team's Creativity, Published by AMACOM Books
American Management Association, www.amanet.org.

141

- Long-Term Perspective

    - _____

    - _____

    - _____

- People Advantage

    - _____

    - _____

    - _____

Innovation at Work: 55 Activities to Spark Your Team's Creativity, Published by AMACOM Books
American Management Association, www.amanet.org.

❖ Scaffolding: ❖
Toward a Culture of Innovation

🕐 *30–60 minutes*

Purpose The purpose of this exercise is to evaluate the personnel in an organization for readiness for innovation.

Materials
- ✓ Worksheet #18
- ✓ Pens
- ✓ Critical, self-reflective eye
- ✓ Laptop computers with Internet access

Procedure
1. Divide the larger group into smaller groups of 4 to 8 participants.

2. Distribute Worksheet #18.

3. Facilitate a discussion of each of the five scaffolds for effective innovation.

   a) **Emotional intelligence.** New innovations require intense collaboration of units, subunits, people, and departments. Innovators have to be able to get along with each other. Emotional intelligence consists of several different facets:
      - Self-awareness
      - Self-management
      - Self-motivation
      - Empathy
      - Social skills

   b) **Innovation skills.** That is what this entire book is about—building different innovation muscles.

   c) **Process training.** Some of this training includes "quality" or "project management" tools: flow charting, value stream mapping, Gantt charts, and the like. The five-step innovation process must also be learned and practiced by employees.

   d) **Motivation.** Sometimes, "we need new products to stay in business" or "we need to speed up our processes to stay competitive" is not enough to motivate employees. Sometimes, contests, prizes, awards, or other kinds of recognitions are needed. Sometimes, in the short run, money is a good incentive.

   e) **Systems thinking.** Employees often need a primer on systems thinking: systems archetypes, systems principles, pattern recognition, and systems failures. Systems thinking is a way of looking at the world, a way that is scaffolding for many disciplines.

Debrief   Scaffolding is an educational concept. Students need to understand Algebra before they move on to Calculus. Students need to complete Spanish I before they move on to Spanish II. The same runs true for innovation. We need to master certain concepts before we can fully engage in others. Yes, there are plenty of examples of lone, eccentric geniuses who rant and rave at others and then invent great projects. Those examples are becoming less and less prevalent. More and more, close creative collaboration creates great innovations. Before diving into innovation projects headlong, organizations should bring their employees up to a certain level of competence in these skills.

Worksheet #18

Scaffolding for Innovation

SCAFFOLD	CURRENT STATE	ACTION STEPS
EMOTIONAL INTELLIGENCE		
INNOVATION TRAINING		
PROCESS TRAINING		
MOTIVATION		
SYSTEMS THINKING		

Innovation at Work: 55 Activities to Spark Your Team's Creativity, Published by AMACOM Books
American Management Association, www.amanet.org.

145

PART 4

The Innovative Process

❖ Open Source Innovation ❖

🕐 *1–4 hours*

Purpose   The purpose of this exercise is to help participants become better observers. People who observe more acutely are more likely to be better innovators.

Materials
- ✓ Notebooks
- ✓ Pens
- ✓ Digital cameras
- ✓ Computer projector
- ✓ Laptop computers
- ✓ Eagle eyes

Procedure

1. This exercise can be done with groups or with individuals.

2. If in groups, divide the larger group into teams. Provide a digital camera to each team.

3. Have each team choose a location to study where consumers consume "something." Send teams out to these locations to observe consumers. Have them take copious pictures of consumers engaged in their tasks. Ask them to observe for an hour or so. Ask them to look for things such as

   a) consumer behaviors;

   b) the way consumers do the work they do;

   c) hassles consumers seem to be having;

   d) jobs that need to be done;

   e) the context of the consumption;

   f) anything else that is interesting.

4. When the teams come back to the seminar location, have them create a PowerPoint from their pictures and notes. They should be ready to tell a story to the larger group about what they saw. Make sure they differentiate between their observations and their inference. (For example, "a person walking into a restaurant" is an observation. "Because they are hungry" is an inference.)

5. Some groups might be confused as to an appropriate place to observe. Examples of places and consumers to observe might be

   a) buyers loading children and groceries into cars in a grocery store parking lot. Maybe the grocery store company wants to make this process easier and safer.

b) people at a baseball game (if you have the time). Maybe the owner of the ball team wants to make the experience a more memorable one.

c) people at a coffee shop—what do they use it for? How can the coffee shop raise the level of that experience?

d) people crossing the streets at a busy urban interaction. How might the city's highway department make the experience safer?

6. Have each team present their insights to the larger group.

Debrief

This can be a powerful and fun exercise. Most participants have been at these places of observation, but have not observed deeply what is happening. They will see things that they have never seen before. They will have new insights. These insights may lead to innovations.

The purpose of this exercise is to promote deep thinking. Make sure that participants can discern the difference between just "casually seeing" and "deeply observing."

Early (1920s) car salesmen observed farmers buying Model T Fords and then immediately tearing the back seats out. This observation led to the creation of a pickup truck. A person observing car drivers holding cups of coffee between their legs created cup holders in cars. (Yes, some of you readers are too young to remember cars without cup holders. But many of us do remember.)

❖ Deep Inquiry ❖

🕐 *60 minutes*

Purpose The purpose of this exercise is to give participants practice in deep inquiry toward the goal of innovation.

Materials ✓ Notebook paper
       ✓ Pens
       ✓ Desire for deep understanding

Procedure 1. This exercise can be done in groups of 2, 3, or 4. Divide the group accordingly.

      2. Ask each participant to think of an activity that they love to do.

      3. Ask the other members of the group to begin to ask the designated person about their hobby or activity. The questions should become progressively deeper. Some questions might be:

        a) How do you feel when you are doing this activity?

        b) This activity is like a _____ when I am engaged in it.

        c) If this activity were an animal, it would be _____.

        d) What do you wish for when you are doing this activity?

        e) Who do you wish to share this activity with?

        f) What is one thing that would make this activity even better?

        g) What do you think about when you are doing this activity?

        h) What deep needs is this activity filling?

      4. After asking these questions for about 20 minutes, stop. Have the small group review the data, and think of any products or services that would make this activity better.

      5. Go on to the next person and do the same kind of questioning. Do this for the time length that you have.

Debrief This exercise helps build the muscle of questioning. Trying to understand deep needs, aspirations, hopes, and dreams can help the process of innovation. The better one understands the psyche, the better one can help fulfill the needs of that psyche through products and services.

❖ Creative Collage Making ❖

⏱ *2–4 hours*

Purpose   The purpose of this exercise is to show how visual stimuli can be used to stimulate innovation.

Materials
- ✓ Old magazines full of pictures
- ✓ Glue sticks
- ✓ Poster boards
- ✓ Markers
- ✓ Scissors
- ✓ Post-it Notes
- ✓ Playfulness
- ✓ Digital cameras (optional)

Procedure

1. Divide the larger group into smaller groups of 4 to 7 participants and let them know that they are going to have fun today.

2. Ask each group to choose a psychographic profile to dive into, for instance:
   a) Suzy, 25-year-old, single, upscale urban professional
   b) George, 67-year-old, retired, living on fixed income with wife in first ring suburb
   c) Joan, 36-year-old, financially struggling, single mom
   d) Sam, 23-year-old, urban graduate student with high aspirations

3. **Phase 1:** Have each group page through the magazines and find pictures of people, products, retail locations, and other artifacts that fit this personage. Have them cut out these pictures and create a collage that tells the story about this psychographic. They might want to write down notes about a day in the life of this individual.

4. Have a representative from each group report out to the larger group. These reports should include things such as
   a) likes and dislikes;
   b) media used;
   c) retail establishments frequented;
   d) dreams and aspirations;
   e) political outlooks.

   Note: This phase might take some imagination. If you were real marketing professionals, you would have hard data and elaborate reports from which to work.

5. After each presentation, have all of the other participants write down one "insightful, brilliant, and probing" question on a Post-it Note. Collect the questions.

6. At the end of the presentations, distribute the Post-it questions to the appropriate groups. The groups discuss the questions among themselves.

7. Phase 2: Back in the smaller groups, each group will develop one to three new product/service offerings for their demographic target. They are to elaborate on these product/service offerings and include

   a) price points;

   b) distribution channels;

   c) marketing strategy;

   d) promotional strategy.

8. Have a member of the small groups report-out to the larger group. Optional: You can have other participants ask elaborating questions to the presenting group.

9. **Variation**: Instead of using magazines, you can send the groups, with digital cameras, out into the world. They can visit stores, restaurants, bus stops, and places like that and take pictures of people who seem to fit their demographic profile. This variation will only work if you are conducting the workshop in an area with many people. Instead of creating a collage, the groups can create a slide show on that personality profile.

Debrief   Debrief questions might include:

- Did you feel like a marketing guru?

- How well did you get into the heads of your psychographic profile?

- Did the visual prompts help your creative process?

- What additional questions would you have for your "Suzy" or "George"?

- What other methods would you employ to get into their heads?

❖ Disassembling ❖

🕐 *1–2 hours*

Purpose   The purpose of this exercise is to build the curiosity of participants.

Materials
- ✓ Flipchart paper (optional)
- ✓ Markers
- ✓ Notebook paper
- ✓ Inquisitive nature
- ✓ Laptop computers with Internet access
- ✓ Old and broken appliances and machines (for example, computers, blenders, light switches, printers, de-humidifiers, microwaves, TVs)
- ✓ Screwdrivers
- ✓ Hammers
- ✓ Pliers
- ✓ Wrench set

Procedure

1. Divide the larger group into smaller groups of 3 to 4 participants.

2. Give each group one or two of the appliances and some tools. Tell them to disassemble the appliances. Their goal is to totally understand how the appliance works. They can use the Internet and the website www.howthingswork.com to help them with this.

3. After they have disassembled and understand their appliances, have a member from each small group explain and describe it to the other members of the larger group.

4. Have the small groups then get back together and study the appliance. What innovation or innovations would make the appliance more effective? What other bells and whistles could be added to make it sexier or better?

5. Have a member from each small group report-out these innovations to the larger group.

6. **Optional:** Have the small groups put the appliances back together and workable. (This might be really fun.)

Debrief   There is no "wrong" way to do this exercise. Participants should have fun. You might ask: What does this have to do with your job? Hopefully they talk about the curiosity to take apart existing processes and ways to do things and look at them with new eyes. One way to innovation is to take apart and totally understand what you currently have in order to improve it or build on it. This is a discipline not solely in the purview of engineers. Innovation is everyone's job.

You may want to mention that if they do this at home to please unplug the appliances before dissassembling.

❖ Question Circle ❖

🕐 *45 minutes*

Purpose   The purpose of this exercise is to allow participants to formulate deep questions. This exercise also allows participants to sit with unanswered questions to their own concerns.

Materials
- ✓ Post-it Notes for everyone
- ✓ Inquisitiveness
- ✓ Laptop computer (optional)

Procedure
1. Rearrange the room so that groups of 10 to 12 participants can sit in circles.

2. Ask each participant to think of a difficult business problem/challenge/dilemma that they are facing. Optional: Have them write the problem down. Allow 3 to 5 minutes of thoughtful silence.

3. Each person will have the opportunity to present his/her question to the group in a circle. As each person presents her/his problem/challenge/dilemma, allow the group several minutes of thoughtful reflection. Members of the group can ask clarifying questions to the presenter.

4. Each person should develop at least one insightful question about the presented problem/challenge/dilemma. They can write them down on Post-it Notes if desired.

5. Then, going around the circle, each person presents their first question. The problem presenter **says nothing.** The presenter just listens and thinks about what she/he is hearing.

6. After one round of the circle, the floor is open for anyone to ask additional questions. This continues until there is silence. The presenter thanks the group, and the group moves on to the next presenter.

7. A scribe could be capturing all of these questions on the laptop to distribute to all of the presenters. Or the presenter could collect the Post-it Notes as a remembering device.

8. Once all of the participants have presented their problems/challenges/dilemmas, have a large group discussion about the process.

Debrief   Ask the larger group how it was to be part of the process. Most presenters probably had a hard time being quiet and not trying to answer the questions. You might mention that often silence breeds thoughtfulness. Also, too often we think that we have the answers when we really do not.

The points of this exercise are to

- learn how to formulate powerful questions;
- build a learning community;
- use astute questioning as part of the innovation process;
- learn to sit with unanswered questions rather than jumping to the punch;
- learn how to be helpful to colleagues.

❖ Deep Empathy ❖

⏱ *2 hours*

Purpose   The purpose of this exercise is to allow participants to be better anthropologists, exploring an important issue for their human friends.

Materials
- ✓ Paper and pens (or laptop computers)
- ✓ An insatiable case of curiosity
- ✓ Worksheet #19
- ✓ Flipchart paper and markers (optional)

Procedure

1. There is not an optimum size for this exercise. Each group should have two sub-groups of at least four participants. There can be many of these groups.

2. Have each group choose who will be the questioners and who will be the subjects. These groups will change roles at each round.

3. Distribute Worksheet #19.

4. Each group must start with one event or experience. Examples might include the following
   a) going to college
   b) having a physical at the doctor's office
   c) going to a professional sports event
   d) going to a parent/teacher meeting at school
   e) shopping for intimate apparel
   f) going to a movie
   g) cooking a three-course meal
   h) attending a wake or funeral
   i) burying a pet

5. The questioners will attempt to understand fully and deeply the participants' needs, desires, wishes, and feelings about taking part in this event or experience.

6. Allow the group 30 minutes. The questioners should jot down notes. At the end of the allotted time, ask each group (two subgroups) to brainstorm new services or products that may enhance this event or experience. Have one group member take notes on this.

7. **Optional:** The questioners may want to organize their data in the following way. Create a 4-quadrant grid on a flip chart page. Label the quadrants: "say," "do," "think," and "feel" and put remarks into one of these categories.

8. Ask the subgroups to switch roles and choose another event or experience. Again, allow the questioning to go on for 30 minutes.

9. At the end of the 30 minutes, allow the group to brainstorm for new product/ service ideas.

Debrief   Ask the participants to reflect on the exercise:

- Was it fun?

- Was it uplifting?

- Did it get them to think in different ways?

- Can they see an application for their organization?

- Did it help them build their curiosity levels?

- Do they think that they dug deeply enough?

- How could they have dug more deeply?

Your final comment might be "Innovators must love people and be curious about them."

Worksheet #19
Probing Questions

1. Describe your highest moment at the event or experience (EE).

2. Describe your lowest moment.

3. Tell a funny story about attending the EE.

4. Were you ever embarrassed at the EE?

5. Did you ever feel sad at the EE? What might have taken that sadness away?

6. When have you known of a friend to have a bad time at the EE? What made it bad/sad/unhappy/ugly?

7. If the EE were an animal, what kind of animal would it be? Why?

8. If you were to redesign the space where the EE happened, how would you do so?

9. If there were a new rule concerning the EE, what would it be?

10. If the EE were a color, what color would it be?

Innovation at Work: 55 Activities to Spark Your Team's Creativity, Published by AMACOM Books
American Management Association, www.amanet.org.

161

❖ Photo Wall ❖

🕐 *1–4 hours*

Purpose   The purpose of this exercise is to show how visuals can be used in the innovation process.

Materials
- ✓ Flipchart paper
- ✓ Markers
- ✓ Tape
- ✓ Wall space
- ✓ Digital cameras (one per person, preferably)
- ✓ Photo printer
- ✓ Photo paper

Procedure

1. This activity can be done in either small or a large group. Each group can choose a different activity or use the same one.

2. Send the group (or groups) out to observe an activity. Possible activities include the following:
   a) grocery shopping
   b) clothes shopping
   c) crossing urban streets
   d) using mass transportation
   e) going to the emergency room at a local hospital
   f) going to a beach or swimming pool
   g) going to a local pub or sports bar
   h) shopping at a mall

3. Have the groups take as many photos as possible of the activity. Have them print the photos, either with a photo printer or at a nearby drugstore or big box store. Have the groups return to the workshop room after a specified time.

4. Have the groups tape their photos on a wall and look at them. If they want, they can organize them how they choose.

5. Have each group label three flipchart pages "what," "how," and "why."

6. Have them fill these flipchart pages from what they see in these photos.

7. Using their photos, their organizational scheme (if they have one), and their flip chart pages, have the groups brainstorm possible innovations for the activity they have taken photos of. For instance, if they have photo-documented a pub, what services or products might make this a richer experience for participants?

8. Have the smaller groups report-out to the larger group.

Debrief Ask participants how the experience went for them. Ask them if they saw things in the photos that they did not see with their own eyes. Discuss how visual images can spark ideas that words or conversation may not be able to.

❖ Can You Hear Me Now? ❖

🕐 *60 minutes*

Purpose   The purpose of this exercise is to show how an organized brainstorming session can lead to actions taken and problems solved.

Materials
- ✓ Flipchart paper
- ✓ Markers
- ✓ Post-it Notes
- ✓ Pens
- ✓ Worksheet #20

Procedure

1. Distribute Worksheet #20.

2. Ask the participants to name some of their organizational problems.

3. One of the issues that will always come up is communication. Typically, the conversation stops there. But what do they mean by poor communication? This exercise gives an opportunity to dig deeper into this issue.

4. Ask the participants to write on Post-It Notes 5–10 specific communication problems in their organization and to stick the Post-it Notes on a wall or on a table.

5. Ask the group to organize the Post-it Notes into themes. This might be chaotic with a larger group, so if it is large, you may want to divide the group into two smaller groups.

6. To do this, you might have them create a flip chart page for each theme and put the appropriate Post-it Notes on the correct flip chart page.

7. When that is accomplished, have each smaller group choose one of the themes (flip chart page with Post-it Notes).

8. Have each of the smaller groups put together a series of action items in order to alleviate the problem. Each action item needs to have a champion, a team, a timeline, and an assessment tactic.

9. Have each of the smaller groups report-out their findings and action steps to the larger group.

Debrief   Some words are becoming cliché-ish in western culture. "Communication" is one of them. This exercise attempts to add meaning to that word. During the debriefing, ask participants how energized they feel. Ask them how doable their action plans seem.

You may want to talk about the entire process of communication. Why is it that we have more communication tools than ever and yet communication often seems worse than ever?

Ask the participants what other organizational problems might be able to be broken into bite-sized pieces and solved.

Worksheet #20
Brainstorming Rules

- Encourage weird ideas

- Focus and refocus on issue

- One conversation at a time

- Build on each other's ideas

- No negative feedback

Innovation at Work: 55 Activities to Spark Your Team's Creativity, Published by AMACOM Books
American Management Association, www.amanet.org.

167

❖ Redesign Rooms ❖

🕐 1 – 4 hours

Purpose
The purpose of this exercise is twofold: to create an innovative space for learning and to give participants a chance to use the process of innovation.

Materials
- ✓ Flipchart paper
- ✓ Markers
- ✓ Notebook paper
- ✓ Colored pencils
- ✓ Rulers
- ✓ Other drawing material, as needed
- ✓ A laptop computer or similar device or two with Internet access for each group

Procedure
1. Divide the larger group into smaller groups of 4 to 7 participants.

2. Tell the groups that their objective is to design a room for maximum learning. Here are the rules:

   a) Money or space is not an issue.

   b) Use any technology that is available.

   c) Use any furniture available—use the Internet to search for future.

   d) Use any resources at hand for ideas.

3. Allow the groups ample time to research and brainstorm and develop their ideas.

4. Have participants report out their final prototype to the larger group. They can use a PowerPoint slide or flipchart pages.

Debrief
After the report-outs, ask the groups to talk about the steps in their process.
- What were the steps they used?
- Which steps seemed to energize? Which steps seemed to deflate?
- Where did they get stuck?
- Did they converge and diverge at times?
- How could they have improved their process?

❖ Two Circle Critique ❖

🕐 *1–2 hours*

Purpose   The purpose of this exercise is to demonstrate a critique process that could lead to an innovation.

Materials   ✓ Flipchart paper
✓ Markers
✓ A product that many people use
✓ A probing sense of curiosity

Procedure   1. Choose a product or service that participants use, have used, or are familiar with. It could be a CD player, the conference room, a blender, a local coffee shop, a flip chart pad, a barber shop. Conversely, you could use a hypothetical product that has not been introduced into the marketplace. It could be in prototype form or sketched out on paper.

2. Divide the larger group into two smaller groups. If the group is too large, create four smaller groups.

3. Have one group create and sit in an inner circle of chairs and the other group should sit in chairs around them.

4. The outer group should have two members standing at flip charts. The flip charts should be divided into four quadrants: green light or positives, red lights or criticisms, mild or wild ideas, and puzzling questions.

5. The outer group should question the inner group about the experience, service, or product. They should probe as deeply as possible. As the inner group responds, the scribes should put the responses in the appropriate boxes.

6. After 20–30 minutes, the entire group should discuss the results. Brainstorm an open discussion about possible innovations based on the grid. How can the product/service/experience be improved?

7. Have the groups reverse the seating so the inner circle becomes the outer circle and vice versa. Redo the process with another product/service/experience.

Debrief   This exercise helps participants build on whatever exists already. Ask the following questions in the debriefing:

- Was it easier to be critical or positive?

- Is it easier doing this exercise in a group? Can you build on each other?

- How easy was it to make the leap from the raw data on the grid to new innovations?

- Did you stifle any ideas or thoughts? Why?

- How could the process have been improved?

❖ Force Field Analysis ❖

⏱ *30–60 minutes*

Purpose The purpose of this exercise is to give participants a tool to use for implementing an innovation or a change.

Materials ✓ Flipchart paper
✓ Markers
✓ Worksheet #21

Procedure 1. Distribute Worksheet #21 to participants.

2. This process, invented by Kurt Levin, is used widely around the world.

3. Divide the larger group into smaller groups of 4 to 7 participants.

4. Each group needs to choose an innovation or change they wish to implement in their organizations.

5. Perform a force field analysis with the participants as an example. The steps are:

a) Choose a change or an innovation (for example, smoking cessation, implementation of a new ERP system, a reorganization, a new billing system)

b) Have the participants name a best-case scenario and worst-case scenario for the change, and write those down.

c) Create a large "T" on a piece of flip chart paper (or use the one on Worksheet #21). Label one column "forces for" and the other "forces against" (the change).

d) Have the participants brainstorm the forces for and the forces against the innovation or change.

e) Then have the participants brainstorm ways to strengthen the forces for the change and weaken the forces against the change

6. After the practice exercise, the small groups can do a force field analysis of their own, choosing their own innovation or change.

7. Have the small groups report out to the larger group.

Debrief   The force field analysis is one of the most popular "organized brainstorming" processes used in the world. It can help groups and individuals prepare for change. It can also help groups and individuals implement a change. Ask participants where this process might be useful in their organizations. Ask them if they think many impediments to changes or innovations can be anticipated. Ask them if they could use this tool for personal changes, like losing weight or stopping smoking or changing some undesirable habit.

Worksheet #21
Force Field Analysis

Best-Case Scenario:

_____

_____

_____

Worst-Case Scenario:

_____

_____

_____

FORCES FOR (+)	FORCES AGAINST (–)

Action Step #1:

_____

Action Step #2:

_____

Action Step #3:

_____

_____

Innovation at Work: 55 Activities to Spark Your Team's Creativity, Published by AMACOM Books
American Management Association, www.amanet.org.

175

❖ Litmus Test ❖

🕐 *30–60 minutes*

Purpose   The purpose of this exercise is to give participants a rudimentary tool with which they can analyze innovations.

Materials   ✓ Paper
                ✓ Pens
                ✓ Worksheet #22
                ✓ Laptop computer with Internet access (optional)

Procedure   1. Divide the larger group into smaller groups of 4 to 7 participants.

                2. Distribute Worksheet #22 to participants.

                3. Explain the purpose of this exercise to the participants. You should discuss each of the criteria for successful innovations on Worksheet #22.

                4. Have each small group choose some innovations and analyze them using these criteria. These innovations can be process innovations, product innovations, imagined innovations, or real innovations.

                5. The smaller groups can report-out to the larger group.

Debrief   You might ask the following questions:

                • Do all of these criteria make sense?

                • In which circumstances might one or more of these not make sense?

                • What other criteria might be valuable?

Worksheet #22
Criteria for Innovations

Understandable

Can potential users easily understand this innovation, or learn how to use it quickly? Board game creators often use this rubric for a new game: Does it only take less than 30 minutes to learn but years to master?

Reversibility

Can the buyer bring it back if it does not suit her/his needs? Is the downside small enough to warrant a try from new users?

Wow Factor

Is this product/service exciting or unusual? Why should people shift from their present product or service? An iPod has a "wow" factor. So does shopping at Trader Joe's, for some people.

Necessary

Does the product/service solve a problem or do an important job? Does it make life easier/better/more efficient/more joyful for its target market?

Context

Does the product have a necessary context? The Segway is a great innovation, but it does not have a necessary context, except for tours or in airports. On the sidewalk, it can run down pedestrians. On city streets, it will be run down.

Innovation at Work: 55 Activities to Spark Your Team's Creativity, Published by AMACOM Books
American Management Association, www.amanet.org.

179

❖ Attribute Listing ❖

🕐 *1–2 hours*

Purpose The purpose of this exercise is to give participants an understanding of another "organized" brainstorming technique.

Materials
- ✓ Flipchart paper
- ✓ Markers
- ✓ Worksheet #23
- ✓ Wild but practical imagination

Procedure

1. Divide the larger group into smaller groups of 4–8 participants.

2. Distribute Worksheet #23.

3. Have each group choose a product or process that they wish to redesign. It should be something real from their workplace or something they are all familiar with, like a bike. Then they will work through the following steps to create a new version of that product or process, using the worksheet:

4. Break that item down into component parts—maybe five to eight of them.

5. Brainstorm six options for each of these components.

6. Choose one option from each component and create a new rendition of the original product.

7. Have the smaller groups report-out their findings to the larger group.

Debrief Have the participants note how this process has both divergent and convergent steps. Both are necessary for innovation. Ask the participants if this process is more productive than unorganized brainstorming. The answer should be yes.

This process can be used later in the innovation process, after much data is gathered by research and observation. It can help put together some disparate pieces into a cohesive whole.

Worksheet #23
Attribute Listing

One way to redesign products or systems is to break them down into component parts, then look at each of the components or steps for choices or options. For instance, let us look at a baby stroller:

- Wheels
- Cover
- Handles
- Storage space
- Seat
- Axles
- Hinges
- Compactable

What options might you have for each of these component parts? List four or five for each and then collect and combine several of these to create a new baby stroller.

Think of another product. List the attributes and brainstorm alternatives for each of the attributes. Use the chart on the following page.

Innovation at Work: 55 Activities to Spark Your Team's Creativity, Published by AMACOM Books
American Management Association, www.amanet.org.

183

Product: _____

ATTRIBUTE	OPTION 1	OPTION 2	OPTION 3	OPTION 4	OPTION 5
1.					
2.					
3.					
4.					
5.					

❖ Blue Ocean Technique ❖

(This technique comes from *Blue Ocean Strategy,* written by Kim and Mauborgne, a best-selling book about innovation and strategy.)

🕐 *1–2 hours*

Purpose   The purpose of this exercise is to give participants the chance to practice blue ocean innovation, a technique for creating new market space for companies.

Materials   ✓ Flipchart paper
                     ✓ Markers
                     ✓ Worksheet #24

Procedure   1. Divide the larger group into smaller groups of 4 to 8 participants.

                     2. Distribute Worksheet #24.

                     3. Explain the theory behind blue ocean strategies. Most companies compete in the red ocean, where competitive sharks are always biting at you and your offerings, drawing blood. This is a tough, competitive environment. Organizations should be innovative and create blue ocean competitive space, where there is not any competition. "Blue ocean" is competitive space where product and service offerings are so different from the competition that the market space is not bloodied.

                     4. One way to look at this competitive space is to work with the grid found in Worksheet #24. Have the participants choose one of their market offerings (product or service) and redesign it. Have them fill in the four quadrants—create, raise, eliminate, reduce. What new attribute can they create for that offering? What attribute could they raise the level of? What could they eliminate? What could they reduce?

                     5. After the participants fill in their grid, have them develop their new product or service concept and then present it to the larger group.

Debrief   "Blue ocean" has become a well-used phrase in corporate America. It is synonymous with finding a new market space where there is no competition. Easier said than done. But, again, this is an organized kind of brainstorming.

You can emphasize that this technique can be used for processes, products, or services. It is similar to questioning assumptions. Why do we need this step? Why does the price need to be this high? Why does this service have to be part of the package?

Example #1
Let's look at an example: Aldi Foods. What has this chain done to be successful?

- *Eliminate:* any frills, any services

- *Reduce:* price, SKUs, loss to aging stock, floor space

- *Raise:* speed of cashiers, corn syrup instead of sugar to lower costs, sales per square foot

- *Create:* price for shopping carts, paper bags

Example #2
Let's look at another example: Trader Joe's (same owner as Aldi).

- **Eliminate:** lost shoppers, corn syrup, grumpy or indifferent employees

- **Reduce:** price, number of SKUs

- **Raise:** own brand of foods, customer service, fun people to help shoppers, team orientation of employees

- **Create:** fun in grocery shopping business, fun website

Worksheet #24
Blue Ocean Technique Grid

Create	Raise
Eliminate	Reduce

Innovation at Work: 55 Activities to Spark Your Team's Creativity, Published by AMACOM Books
American Management Association, www.amanet.org.

187

❖ Club Med Exercise ❖

🕐 *30–60 minutes*

Purpose   The purpose of this exercise is to give participants another organized brainstorming technique to use when innovating services.

Materials
- ✓ Flipchart paper
- ✓ Markers
- ✓ Worksheet #25

Procedure

1. This format has been used by Club Med, the resort company, with all of their services.

2. Divide the larger group into smaller groups of 4 to 7 participants.

3. Distribute Worksheet #25.

4. Have each group choose a process (set of steps) that their customers go through to do business with them. For example:

   a) entering, being seated, and ordering at a restaurant

   b) being billed and making a payment

   c) renting a car and returning it

5. Have the groups walk through the three steps from Worksheet #25:

   a) What are the steps in the process?

   b) At each step, what possibly could go wrong?

   c) To prevent each of these things from going wrong, what could the organization do, in terms of people, materials, and policies, to prevent them from going wrong?

6. Have the smaller groups report-out their findings to the larger group. The rest of the participants can add to their list of preventative measures.

Debrief   You can summarize the exercise by asking the following questions:

- How does this exercise relate to a standard flowchart? (It is a flowchart from the perspective of a customer.)

- Could any steps be added to improve this process?

- In some cases, could the preventative fixes be more expensive than the problems that may be created?

Worksheet #25
Club Med Exercise

What are the steps in the process?

1. _____
2. _____
3. _____
4. _____
5. _____
6. _____

At each step, what possibly could go wrong?

1. _____
2. _____
3. _____
4. _____
5. _____
6. _____

To prevent each of these things from going wrong, what could the organization do, in terms of people, materials, and policies, to prevent them from going wrong?

1. _____
2. _____
3. _____
4. _____
5. _____
6. _____

Innovation at Work: 55 Activities to Spark Your Team's Creativity, Published by AMACOM Books
American Management Association, www.amanet.org.

191

❖ Designing an Innovation Room ❖

🕐 *1½–2 hours*

Purpose   The purpose of this exercise is for participants to design a physical space where methodical innovation can happen.

Materials
- ✓ Flipchart paper
- ✓ Markers
- ✓ Notebook paper
- ✓ Pens
- ✓ Laptop computers with Internet access
- ✓ Vivid imagination
- ✓ Worksheet #26

Procedure
1. More and more companies are creating innovation rooms. These rooms provide a space for groups to brainstorm and work with ideas that they wish to bring to fruition. These rooms typically have walls made of white board material. Depending on how big the room is, there are many other items to be used in the innovation process.

2. Divide the larger group into smaller groups of 6 to 8 participants. Explain their goal—design an innovation room. If this workshop is taking place at a corporation and groups know of a room that would serve this purpose well, they might go and look at it. They also might use the Internet to find examples of innovation rooms.

3. Distribute Worksheet #26.

4. The groups might use organized brainstorming techniques like SCAMPER or Attribute Listing to perform this task.

5. Have the groups create something to present to the larger group. It may be sketches or a blueprint. It may be a PowerPoint. It may be a list of items that would be kept in bins in the innovation room (see Worksheet #26).

Debrief   You should ask some of these questions:
- What makes for a creative space?
- Can you ensure that innovation will happen?
- What materials help the creative process? Which hinder?
- What kinds of desks and chairs are best for creativity enhancement?
- What is the best way to capture all of the ideas?

Worksheet #26
Innovation Room Enhancers

Play dough

Pipe cleaners

Markers, pens, crayons, scissors, other school supplies

3″ x 5″ cards

Post-it Notes

Bin full of broken parts
- light fixtures
- on/off switches
- old toys
- metal pieces
- tools
- kitchen implements
- etc.

Books about innovation

Yard stick

Poster boards

Glue, tape, duct tape, and other adhesives

Old magazines with pictures

Computer projector

Copious dark chocolate (helps with serotonin enhancement)

Innovation at Work: 55 Activities to Spark Your Team's Creativity, Published by AMACOM Books
American Management Association, www.amanet.org.

195

❖ SCAMPER ❖

🕐 *30–60 minutes*

Purpose   The purpose of this exercise is to introduce participants to an organized brainstorming technique entitled SCAMPER.

Materials   ✓ Flipchart paper
✓ Markers
✓ A sense of humor
✓ A deck of "scamper" cards (optional)

Procedure   1. Introduce the participants to the acronym SCAMPER:
- **S**ubstitute
- **C**ombine
- **A**dapt
- **M**inimize, maximize
- **P**ut to other uses
- **E**laborate, eliminate
- **R**everse, rearrange

2. Explain to the participants that this is an organized brainstorming technique.

3. To warm up participants, give them some funny items with which to work. Ask them what they could do with the following things to make them useful or profitable:
- dry Christmas trees in early January
- moldy pumpkins after Halloween
- obsolete tanks at the end of the Cold War
- 1,000 leftover bricks
- 6 tons of ball bearings
- an abandoned factory in Detroit
- 10 retired lawyers

4. Have each group tackle several of these using the SCAMPER method, taking each step in order. Have each group develop two creative innovations for each of the items.

5. The smaller groups will report-out to the larger group and have the larger group vote on each of the innovations.

6. This can be used as a warm-up exercise. At this point, you may move the group into a real innovation exercise. For instance, ask the groups to use SCAMPER to develop innovative uses for some internal issues:

- excess capacity in the advertising department

- pounds of excess shipping material

- hundreds of discarded shipping pallets

- 300 old cubicle dividers

- 500 volunteer hours

- 10 retired executives who are bored

Debrief   SCAMPER is an old and tested technique. It can be used in a variety of situations. Ask participants if they came up with more ideas because of the prompts. The purpose of the scamper prompts is to spur creativity.

Posters and Quotes

50 Innovation Techniques: Addendums

Probe the Constituency	• In this step, innovators identify who the client is, what the new IT is, what the constraints are, and what research and resources are necessary to become informed. The goal of this step is to gain full understanding of the issue(s).
Observe the Real Situation	• Through observation, innovators observe real world application of the issue. The observation should be focused on what makes the customer tick and what confuses and confounds. • Mountains of data are gathered during this phase of the process.
Develop New Concepts	• Developing new concepts can be defined in one word: *brainstorming.* This step of the process calls for any and all ideas to be generated and shared, as Brynteson says, both the "outlandish" and "impractical."
Converge and Build Prototypes	• Brainstorming ideas are distilled down into workable prototypes. • The good and bad are weighed, and decisions are made.
Implementation Process	• The central question here is, "How do we put this new process/procedure into action?"

Step #1: Probe the Constituency:
Questions to Consider

- How do others do the task?

- What are their constraints?

- What other technologies can be employed here?

- Name five other processes that this process is like.

- Name five other processes that this process is *not* like, but may be appropriate, with the use of a little imagination.

- What box can we step out of?

- What possible boxes can we step into?

- What is the history of this process? Has the history been linear or discontinuous?

- What has worked well? What has not?

- What is customer input?

- Who are all of the constituencies?

- What are the formal feedback mechanisms?

- In an ideal world, what would they want?

- Draw realistic pictures.

- Draw unrealistic pictures.

- What are the assumed constraints of the project?

- What other secondary data are available but not explored?

Step #2: Observe the Real Situation:
Questions to Consider

- Where can you find people using this process or system?

- Can you observe them without them changing their behavior?

- What method is best for documenting what you see?
  - ✓ digital camera
  - ✓ video camera
  - ✓ copious field notes (with a laptop)
  - ✓ paper and pencil
  - ✓ other

- What kinds of questions can you use to obtain the deepest information?

- Are there other ways of obtaining information that you haven't thought of?

- Watch users using the process.

- Observe data trends.

- Observe users of data.

- What is the information used for?

- How can this information be more accessible and more useful?

- What confounds and confuses customers?

- What feedback loops are in place that would make this more of a learning organization?

- Do a data dump/synoptic learning mind map to collect and disseminate the data.

- Take pictures.

- Do interviews.

- Take copious field notes.

Step #3: Develop New Concepts:
Questions to Consider

- Are we stretching ourselves far enough?

- What boxes have we forgotten?

- What other boxes do we need to enter?

- What connections have not been made?

- What voices are not being heard? What voices are minimized?

- Was convergence too fast?

- What are the unintended consequences of the new prototype?

- How engaged are the participants?

- When are they engaged? Not engaged?

- Are there wacky enough ideas?

Step #4: Converge and Build Prototypes: Questions to Consider

- Is the focus in the right place?

- Can the group poke fun at their own prototypes?

- Is there an atmosphere of friendly competition?

- What are the unintended consequences of each of the prototypes?

- Use Post-it Notes to vote.

- Can we disassemble and reassemble the prototypes?

- What is at stake for each of the prototypes?

- Do we have aliens in the group?

- Are there deliberate provocateurs?

- How can we improve on it?

- In what ways might we...?

- Is everyone engaged? If not, why not?

- What questions are not being asked?

- Are all of the constituencies being represented?

- What will work best given the primary clients of this organization?

Step #5: Implementation Process:
Questions to Consider

- Do a force field analysis.

- Who will lose if this innovation is accepted?

- Who will win if this innovation is accepted?

- What are organizational impediments?

- What are individual impediments?

- What action planning is useful?

- What is organizational readiness?

- What are the unintended consequences of this?

Categories of Innovation

- Process improvement ideas (lean manufacturing, Six Sigma)

- Derivative ideas (Starbucks, microloans)

- Breakthrough ideas (*Harry Potter,* space travel)

- Radical innovations (iPods, wireless)

Accident as Innovation

"Accident is the name of the greatest of all inventors."
—Mark Twain

Example #1

In 1928, Alexander Fleming left a window open next to a petri dish with a colony of bacteria. He came back the next morning. He looked through a microscope at his ruined experiment. He saw mold destroying the bacteria. He invented penicillin. The formula: accident plus acute observation.

Example #2

Percy Lebaron Spencer had 120 patents, mostly in the defense industry. One day, he walked by a magnetron—a machine used in radar. A chocolate candy bar in his pocket melted. He grabbed a handful of popcorn kernels and put them in front of the magnetron—they popped! The formula: accident plus observation plus experimentation.

Example #3

Eleven-year-old Frank Epperson left a mixture of soda powder and water; it froze to a mixing stick. Twenty years later, he decided to add some flavors, and lo and behold we had the "Eppsicles." The name needed some refinement: Popsicles. He received royalties for 60 million of them. The formula: accident plus memory plus experimentation.

"There's no use trying," Alice said; "one can't believe impossible things."

"I daresay you haven't had much practice," said the Queen. "When I was younger, I always did it for half an hour a day. Why, sometimes I've believed as many as six impossible things before breakfast."

From *Alice in Wonderland*

Not an inventor?

- The ballpoint pen was invented by a sculptor.

- The parking meter was invented by a journalist.

- The Wright brothers were bike mechanics, not aeronautical engineers.

- Kodachrome film was developed by a musician.

"There is nothing more difficult to carry out, nor more doubtful of success, nor more dangerous to handle, than to initiate a new order of things. For the reformer has enemies in all those that profit by the old order, and only lukewarm defenders in all those who would profit by the new order, this lukewarmness arising…partly from the incredulity of mankind, **who do not truly believe in anything new until they have had actual experience of it.**"

—Niccolo Machiavelli, *The Prince,* 1513

"Creativity is the ability to look at the ordinary, and see the extraordinary."

—Dewitt Jones

"Success is the ability to go from failure to failure without losing your enthusiasm."

—Winston Churchhill

"From cradle to grave the pressure is on: BE NORMAL… The trouble with this is that corporate normalcy derives from and is dedicated to past realities and past successes. There is no room for…original thinking."

—Tom Peters

"The act of experimenting sets up a virtuous cycle of innovation; this cycle can constitute such a dominant characteristic of the organization that the ability to experiment and prototype efficiently and competently itself constitutes a competitively advantageous capability."

—Dorothy Leonard-Barton,
Wellsprings of Knowledge, p. 114

"Innovation requires a fresh way of looking at things, an understanding of people, and an entrepreneurial willingness to take risks and to work hard. An idea doesn't become an innovation until it is widely adopted and incorporated into people's daily lives. Most people resist change, so a key part of innovating is convincing other people that your idea is a good one—by enlisting their help, and, in doing so, by helping them see the usefulness of the idea."

—Art Fry, Corporate Scientist, 3M
Fast Company, April 2000, p. 100

"We have identified a 'third place.' And I really believe that sets us apart. The third place is that place that's not work or home. It's the place our customers come for refuge."

—Nancy Orsolini, District Manager
Starbucks

Innovation Cases

Navy Patrol Boats

The Problem:

It was very difficult to move heavy electronic equipment in and out of the holds of small Navy patrol boats. These patrol boats were designed and built before sophisticated electronics equipment was used for tracking other ship movements. These patrol boats were being used by an Asian country to intercept gun runners and El Quaida operatives. The vertical passageways were narrow and difficult to maneuver. In moving this heavy electronic equipment, many sailors experienced back and shoulder problems.

The Solution:

A group of sailors, led by innovation consultants, studied the problem extensively. Pairs of the sailors attempted to find other "boxes" that might hold answers. For instance, one group looked into robotics for an answer. They found a robotic device on the market that climbs and descends stairs with heavy loads.

Coincidentally, a cave-in at a subway construction site in an Asian country trapped several of the workers. Emergency teams worked to free these men from under the rubble. They used compact tripods with heavy-duty ropes and pulleys that could be set up anywhere. This mechanism folded up into a duffle bag and could lift in excess of 500 pounds.

Both of these solutions evolved from "getting into another box," not reinventing the wheel. Innovation does not have to be exclusively inventing something new. The world is abundant with solutions—we just need to find the right one for the problem at hand. In this case, the tripod/ropes/pulley options was much more portable and cost-effective than high tech or robotic solutions.

Air Force: Missing Tools

The Problem:

Crews frequently maintained F-17 fighter jets for an Asian Air Force. If, after the jets took off on a mission, a tool could not be found, the jets were summoned back to the airbase, often at great expense. The fear was that the tool might have been left in the engine. A tool rattling around in an engine might bring the plane down in a crash.

The current inventory system for tools was simple yet cumbersome. Tools were checked out by hand and entered in a log system in long hand. It often took 20 minutes. Likewise when the tools were turned in, they were logged in, long hand. It became more complex when multiple tools were checked out quickly or checked back in quickly. One might be left out on either side of the process. If so, a decision had to be made on whether to scramble the aircraft back to the airbase.

The Solution:

A team of airmen, led by innovation consultants, created a check-in, check-out system, with radio-frequency identification (RFID) tags, that made tracking the tools much simpler and time-effective. In order to arrive at this solution, the airmen had to look at parallel processes. They examined library systems and package tracking systems. Although this system required an upfront investment, it could be used for other issues at this airbase and was adopted to do so.

Infantry: Night Vision Goggles

The Problem:

Very expensive night vision goggles were disappearing from the infantry of an Asian country. Some feared that they had fallen into El Quaida hands. Others thought they were being sold by underpaid soldiers on the black market. Others believed that they had just fallen off soldiers and had been lost in swamps during thick jungle maneuvers. Whatever the case, these precision goggles were too expensive to be lost on a regular basis.

The Solution:

An infantry team, facilitated by innovation consultants, thoroughly investigated the issue. One of their first actions was to have a video taken of an infantryman affixing the goggles to his helmet. The process took almost eight minutes as they used hard plastic twist ties to attach the goggles and then trimmed the ends. The team was appalled as they watched the video several times. Note that this was the best way for the team to get into the real situation—they needed to observe the entire process in order to understand it.

The team then broke down the problem into component parts: storing the device, attaching the device, and finding the device when lost. For the first issue, the team consulted a seamstress for a redesign on the infantryman's vest. She helped create a robust pocket with a Velcro and snapping system to ensure that the goggles would not fall out.

The team turned its attention to the attachment problem. The team, with the help of an engineer, devised a clipping system for the helmet. Although this solution required a clipping system for both the helmet and the goggles, it was felt that the incremental expense was well worth the additional security. Finally, the team examined the issue of lost goggles. It looked at several honing devices and flashing light devices. This issue was complicated by the fact that the devices should not be able to be seen by the enemy at night or during the day. Many of these tracking devices could possibly give away troop movement and locations. The team settled on an RFID tracking system with small chips embedded in the helmets.

In the case of these disappearing goggles, breaking the problem into component parts (similar to Attribute Listing) provided the best process for innovation. Each of the three components needed different innovative approaches.

Infantry: Carrying Too Much Weight

The Problem:

Infantry personnel in a small Asian country performed operations in the jungle at 90-degree temperatures and 90 percent humidity. During the course of these operations, several soldiers passed away from carrying too much weight in these difficult conditions. In particular, those who died were carrying very heavy rocket propelled grenade launchers and the rockets for them.

One of the issues faced by the innovation team was the nature of the real problem. Was the real problem how to distribute the weight of all of this equipment or was it that there was too much weight? Some research indicated that men under these conditions cannot possibly carry that much weight.

The Solution:

A team of infantrymen and innovation consultants, with the help of an ergonomics expert and a backpack manufacturer, worked together to find a safer way to carry the weight. They created a backpack and strap system that made carrying large amounts of weight easier.

Live Fire Zone

The Problem:

In live ammunitions night maneuvers, infantrymen could not determine whether they hit their targets. If they did not hit the target, they could not move ahead to the next target. An ancillary problem was that some of the expensive targets were destroyed by 50mm machine gun fire.

A team from the officer training school and an innovation consultant studied the problem by immersing themselves in the real situation. They walked the live fire zone, studied the targets, and observed the maneuvers. They studied how the most sophisticated armies of the world dealt with this problem.

The Solution:

The team discovered a 3M reflective tape that could be used on low-tech targets and that glowed in the dark if hit. Low-tech targets were not damaged by 50mm bullets. Mission accomplished: the team saved money on the targets and found an effective way for soldiers to discern whether they had hit the targets.

Chinook Helicopters: Hydraulic System

The Problem:

Chinooks are large helicopters used for carrying heavy equipment like jeeps and armored cars. They can land equipment in battle zones quickly for fast deployment. The testing time for one small army for the hydraulic systems of Chinook helicopters was 3.5 hours, far too long. In other words, the hydraulic system that dropped a heavy chain and picked up the cargo needed to be tested frequently. A three and a half hour turnaround time for the tests was unrealistic in wartime.

The Solution:

A military team, led by innovation consultants, decided to try to "get into other boxes." In teams of two, they studied other types of hydraulic systems, either in person or through www.howthingswork. com. They examined automobile hydraulic systems, elevator hydraulics, and the cranes that unloaded containers from freight ships. Their investigations indicated that there were many ways to test hydraulics. They found one process that was simple and effective. It ultimately only took 30 minutes to test the hydraulics of these helicopters.

A New Television Program

The Problem:

A major television network needed some new hit shows.

The Solution:

A team of producers and other creative types from the network gathered with an innovation consultant at a resort for two days. Some of the creative processes that the group undertook included the following:

The group conducted a brainstorming session based on data and statistics in order to determine which demographics were the prime targets for new shows. This dive into the data yielded tweens, young professionals, seniors, and stay-at-home mothers.

The group was split into four smaller groups, each representing one of those demographics. Each small group did a "25 questions," where they delineated 25 questions that they have about that demographic. They then researched those questions, using the Internet, public documents, and previous market research conducted by the network. The groups then did a data dump around their demographics.

Each group then developed three to four scenarios for new programs based on their data dump. They weighed the pros and cons of each possibility. After evaluating each option, each group chose one program option.

Each group developed the main characters and plot lines, mapped the first three episodes for their program, and created a set of storyboards to present to the rest of the group.

Notice that this two-day ideation session combined divergent and convergent thinking to capture optimum solutions.

New Corporate Processes

The Problem:

A large multinational computer company had opened a new facility in an Asian country. It was adding new personnel quickly and needed to add more. Because of the fast growth, the culture was in flux and not developing the depth of the corporate culture at headquarters.

The Solution:

A group of managers and an innovation consultant broke the culture problem into four manageable components:

- Recruiting 600 new highly skilled people
- Developing an onboarding process
- Creating a happy, fulfilling workplace
- Developing an innovative culture

Teams took ownership of each of these problems. Teams decided to dig deeply into each of these issues by examining what best-in-class companies do about these issues. Members of the teams interviewed employees in other high-tech companies. They researched the Internet and read case studies. Each team developed a multitude of initiatives to solve their problem. The initiatives were evaluated for feasibility and then ranked. Some were put on the front burner. Others were put on the back burner. Action plans were created for the front burner items.

References

Amabile, T.M. 1998,. "How to kill creativity." *Harvard Business Review*. (September/October): 77-87.

Barker, J. (2001). *The Business of Paradigms*. St. Paul, MN: Star Thrower Distribution.

Barker, J. (2005). *Five regions of the future*. London: Penguin.

Barker, J. (2009). *Innovation at the verge*. St. Paul, MN: Star Thrower Distribution.

"Best Innovations of 2007." (November 12, 2007).*Time magazine*.

Bughin, J., Chui, M., & Johnson, B. (2008) "The next step in innovation." McKinsey Quarterly.

Carter, S. (1999). *Renaissance management: The rebirth of energy and innovation in people and organizations*. London: Kogan Page Limited.

Chowder, K. (September 2003). "Eureka." *Smithsonian Magazine*, p. 92.

Christensen, C. M. (1997). *The innovator's dilemma: When new technologies cause great firms to fail*. Boston: Harvard Business School Press.

Collins, J. (2001). *From good to great*. New York: HarperBusiness.

Drucker, P. (1985). *Innovation and entrepreneurship: Practice and principles*. New York: Harper and Row.

Drucker, P. (August 2002). "The Discipline of Business." *Harvard Business Review*.

Freidel, R. (October 1996). "The accidental inventor." *Discover Magazine*, p. 69.

Fry, A. (April 2000). *Fast Company Magazine*.

Gelb, M. (2007). *Innovate like Edison*. New York: Dutton.

Goleman, D. (1995). Emotional intelligence. New York: Bantam.

Gryskiewicz, S. S. (1999). *Positive turbulence: Developing climates for creativity, innovation and renewal*. San Francisco, CA: Jossey-Bass.

Hamel, G. (February 2006). "The why, what, and how of management innovation." *Harvard Business Review*, pp. 72–84.

Hargadon, A., & Sutton, R.I. (May-June 2000). "Building an innovation factory." *Harvard Business Review*.

Hargadon, A. (2003). *How breakthroughs happen: The surprising truth about how companies innovate*. Boston: Harvard Business School Press.

Heath, C., & Heath, D. (2007). *Made to stick*. New York: Random House.

Kim, W. C., & Mauborgne, R. (2005). Cambridge: Harvard Business School Press.

Leonard, D., & Rayport, J. F. (November–December 1997). "Spark innovation through empathetic design." *Harvard Business Review*.

Leonard-Barton, D. (1995). *Wellsprings of knowledge: Building and sustaining the sources of innovation*. Boston: Harvard Business School Press.

McKinsey and Co. (2007). "How companies approach innovation." 2007 McKinsey on Innovation.

McKinsey and Co. (2010). "Open source innovation" (working paper).

References

Michalko, M. (1991). Thinkertoys. Berkeley: Ten Speed Press.

Miller, W. C. (1998). *Flash of brilliance: Inspiring creativity where you work.* Reading, MA: Perseus Books.

Pink, D. (2005). *A whole new mind.* New York: Riverhead Books.

"Powers of creation." (October 1996). *Discover Magazine.*

Schrage, M. (1989). *No more teams.* New York: Doubleday.

Senge, P. (1990). *The fifth discipline.* New York: Currency Doubleday.

Smith, F. (April 2000). *Fast Company.*

Stacey, R. D. (1996). *Complexity and creativity in organizations.* San Francisco, CA: Berrett-Koehler Publishers Inc.

Tapscott D., and Williams, A. (2010). *Wikinomics: How mass collaboration changes everything.*

"The power of invention." (Winter 1997-1998). *Newsweek Extra.*

Weick, K. E. (1996). "Drop your tools: An allegory for organizational studies." *Administrative Science Quarterly,* p. 2.

Index

Index

About the Author

Richard Brynteson, Ph.D.

"Richard will push your thinking." As an organizational consultant, executive coach, teacher, and writer, Richard helps his students and clients examine their own thinking and make changes in order to improve their productivity and quality of life.

Richard helps his clients innovate work processes and products in order to improve effectiveness and efficiency. He helps his coaching clients explore the relevance of their own assumptions and paradigms. Richard shines a mirror at his coaching clients so they can see the flaws in their thinking.

Richard has helped the Singapore military redesign work systems around Chinook helicopters, F-16 fighter planes, and Naval patrol boats. He has created leadership training programs for several companies, and helped engineers become more personable, executives become less fearful, and managers become more thoughtful.

Representative Clients

Department of Defense, Singapore, Dell Computers, McCann Erickson, Rochester Public Utilities, Austin Utilities, Healtheast, Zumbro Valley Mental Health Centers, Firstmark Services, Medtronic, and various government agencies in the U.S. and abroad.

Professional Background

Professor of Organizational Management, Concordia University (current)
Innovation Consultant, Singapore and Kuala Lumpur
Ecolab, Product Line Manager
Software Clearing House, Marketing Manager
W.R. Grace, Marketing Manager and Financial Analyst

Education

University of Minnesota, Ph.D., Adult Education, 1997
University of Chicago, MBA, Finance and Marketing, 1980
Dartmouth College, BA, English, 1977

> *"Pushing the thinking of individuals and groups… innovation is the driving force of the economy and we can all be innovators."*

Publications

Once Upon a Complex Time: Using Stories to Understand Systems. 2006. www.sparrowhawkmedia.com

The Manager's Pocket Guide to Innovation. 2010, HRD Press, Amherst, MA

The Manager's Pocket Guide to Social Media. (with Carol Rinkoff and Jason DeBoer Moran). 2011, HRD Press, Amherst, MA